UNDERSTANDING
WILD
FLOWERS

Ros Evans

**Illustrated by
Victoria Goaman**

CONTENTS

Edited and designed by Karen Goaman

Additional illustrations by
Julie Piper, John Sibbick, Will Giles and Sally Burrough

The illustrations on pages 41 and 49 in this book have been
previously published in the Usborne Regional Guides.

The author wishes to thank Colin and Penny Legg,
and Hilary Scott, for their help on this book.

First published in 1982 by Usborne Publishing Limited,
20 Garrick Street, London WC2E 9BJ

Made and Printed in Great Britain
by Blantyre Printing and Bookbinding Ltd., London and Glasgow.

The name Usborne and the device 🌐 are Trade Marks of Usborne Publishing Ltd.

INTRODUCTION

Wherever you go, the countryside is covered with plants of various shapes and sizes. The most successful and dominant of these are the flowering plants and, without them, all other forms of life on earth today would not exist.

When these plants bloom, they provide a beautiful range of countless colours, shapes and scents. The flower represents a very important stage in the life cycle of these plants, since it is through the flower that each generation begins.

How to use this book

The first part of this book concentrates on the flower and its purpose and why there are so many different designs even though they all have the same purpose – to reproduce the species.

The second part may help to explain some of the similarities you may notice between certain flowers. Though the book is not an identification guide, the descriptions of families and in particular the key on pages 32–34, should give you a short cut to identifying a flower.

You will probably have noticed some of the characteristic flowers of certain habitats – for instance the primroses, and bluebells which carpet woodland floors in spring. The third part of this book considers the characteristic flowers which you could look out for in different kinds of places (habitats), and begins to answer the question of why they have chosen to grow in these places rather than others.

As you get to know more about flowers, you may want to make closer observations out in the countryside. There are some suggestions for ways of looking at flowers and recording what you see on pages 58–59.

If you come across a term you do not understand, look it up in the index. It may have been explained earlier in the book, usually on the first page listed in the index.

▼ **Purple loosestrife, meadowsweet and hemlock may be found beside rivers and streams.**

THE PURPOSE OF FLOWERS

Parts of a flower

The flower is the centre of a flowering plant's sex life. The flower contains the male and female sex organs, which produce the sex cells. When these fuse, a seed forms and a new generation begins.

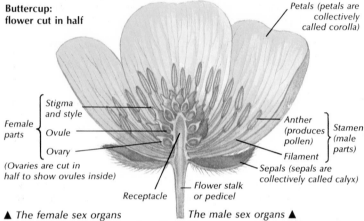

Buttercup:
flower cut in half

Petals (petals are collectively called corolla)

Female parts {
Stigma and style
Ovule
Ovary
}

(Ovaries are cut in half to show ovules inside)

Anther (produces pollen)
Filament
} Stamen (male parts)

Sepals (sepals are collectively called calyx)

Receptacle

Flower stalk or pedicel

▲ The female sex organs
The *ovary* produces the *female cells*. The ovary also encloses the cells to protect them.

The male sex organs ▲
The *anthers* of the *stamens* produce the *male cells*, each one protected in a pollen grain.

From flower to fruit
In all flowers, it is the ovary which develops into a fruit containing one or more seeds. The male and female cells of the same or different plants of the same species must fuse in order to produce a seed. The fusion is called fertilization (see page 8). For fertilization to occur, pollen must first be transferred from the anther of a stamen (male) to the stigma of an ovary (female). This process is called pollination. Pollination may be carried out by the wind, or by insects visiting the flower in search of food (see pages 9–14).

Buttercup: after fertilization

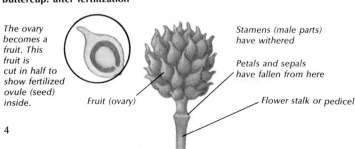

The ovary becomes a fruit. This fruit is cut in half to show fertilized ovule (seed) inside.

Fruit (ovary)

Stamens (male parts) have withered

Petals and sepals have fallen from here

Flower stalk or pedicel

Parts of a flower and their functions

Although sexual reproduction is the main function of all flowers, in many, the sexual organs (stamens and ovaries) are hardly noticeable. This is because the other parts of the flower take on the role of protecting the sexual organs and of attracting insects to visit them, so that pollination is carried out.

The *sepals* (collectively called the *calyx*) are usually small and green and are sometimes fused together. Their main purpose is to protect the flower while it is in bud.

The *petals* (collectively called the *corolla*) are often fused together. They are usually large and attractive in shape, colour and scent, in order to advertise the flower to insect-pollinators. The petals often pro- duce nectar, a sweet liquid which insects love to drink. Nectaries – the glands which produce nectar – are sometimes found on the receptacle or other parts of the flower instead.

Occasionally the sepals are the attractive parts. The petals can then concentrate on nectar production (see winter aconite below).

Numbers of ovaries and ovules

In some plants like the buttercup and bramble, the flowers have sev- eral ovaries, each with a single ovule. In others such as lupin, the flower contains a single ovary with several ovules, each of which, once fertilized, develops into a seed. In some species such as bellflower, the ovaries are fused together (see below).

▼ Petals often produce nectar, the sweet liquid attractive to insects.

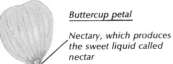

Buttercup petal

Nectary, which produces the sweet liquid called nectar

▼ In some flowers the sepals instead of the petals are coloured. Winter aco- nite has shiny yellow sepals which serve to attract insects, and the petals are tubular nectaries.

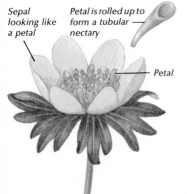

Sepal looking like a petal

Petal is rolled up to form a tubular nectary

Petal

▼ Lupin flower, cut in half, showing the single ovary containing several ovules.

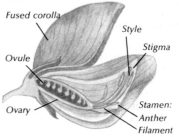

Fused corolla

Style

Stigma

Ovule

Ovary

Stamen:
Anther
Filament

▼ Bellflower, cut in half, showing ovaries and styles fused together.

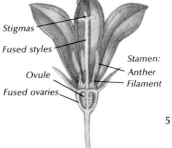

Stigmas

Fused styles

Ovule

Fused ovaries

Stamen:
Anther
Filament

Inflorescences

Surprisingly enough, very few plants bear single flowers. Most flowers are borne in a characteristic arrangement or *inflorescence*. This may look haphazard but in fact each species always sticks to its own pattern of inflorescence, which has a particular purpose. All types of inflorescence have the same aims – to hold the flowers in the most suitable position for pollination and for seed dispersal, and to extend the flowering period.

Once you start looking at inflorescences, you will find a great variety from species to species, and yet some interesting similarities between species even of different families. When you are trying to identify a flower, it is helpful to draw the type of inflorescence as well as the flower. The most common types of inflorescence are shown on these two pages.

(Note: *Peduncle* means the stalk which bears the whole inflorescence. *Pedicel* means the stalk which bears the single flower.)

Raceme

▲ One type of inflorescence is the *raceme*. The flowers, each on its own pedicel, occur at intervals in a spiral up the peduncle. The foxglove above is an example of a raceme. A catkin is also a raceme, often hanging upside down.

▼ One of the most confusing inflorescences is the *head* or *capitulum*. The clustering of flowers together looks just like a single flower. In fact, as shown in the magnifying glass below, the flower head is made up of hundreds of tiny flowers. Each single flower is equipped with its own male and female sexual organs and each is capable of producing a seed.

Most members of the daisy family (Compositae), like the ox-eye daisy shown below, have this type of inflorescence.

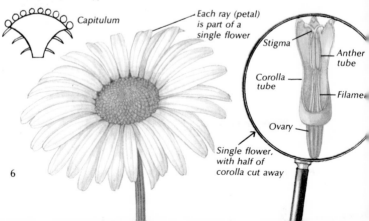

Capitulum

Each ray (petal) is part of a single flower

Stigma

Anther tube

Corolla tube

Filament

Ovary

Single flower, with half of corolla cut away

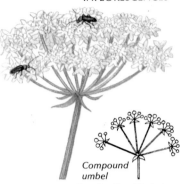

Compound umbel

Umbel

▲ In some flowers all the pedicels grow from the tip of the peduncle. This forms a cluster which may be held up, as in ramsons, or droop, as in cowslip above. This type of inflorescence is called an *umbel*.

▲ The cow parsley family (Umbelliferae) bear *compound umbels*. This is really an umbel of umbels (see cowslips), since the peduncle branches before bearing umbels. The umbels are often flat-topped to provide a platform for insect-pollinators to land on. Some insects also use the platform as a place to display to attract mates, like the soldier beetles on the hogweed above.

▼ Another type of inflorescence is the *cyme*. Here, instead of pedicels growing from the peduncle, the peduncle itself produces a flower so it cannot grow any further. The side branches therefore carry on the growth. But they too end in flowers so *their* side branches must continue the growth.

The red campion (left) is a common example of a cyme. In the forget-me-not (right), the inflorescence starts with two side branches just as in red campion. From then on there is only one side branch each time, and it is always produced on the same side, so the inflorescence stalk becomes coiled.

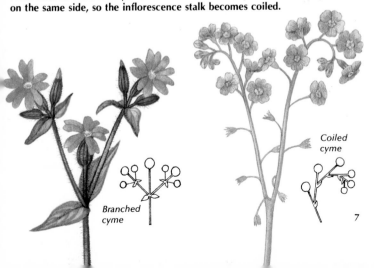

Branched cyme

Coiled cyme

7

Sexual reproduction

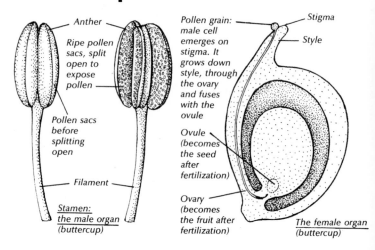

Anther

Ripe pollen sacs, split open to expose pollen

Pollen sacs before splitting open

Filament

Stamen: the male organ (buttercup)

Pollen grain: male cell emerges on stigma. It grows down style, through the ovary and fuses with the ovule

Ovule (becomes the seed after fertilization)

Ovary (becomes the fruit after fertilization)

Stigma

Style

The female organ (buttercup)

▲ Before fertilization can take place – that is the fusing together of male and female cells – the pollen grain must first be transferred from the male anther to the receptive *stigma* of a female ovary. This process is called *pollination*.

The male cell emerges from the pollen grain on the surface of the stigma, and penetrates the ovary wall. It passes down through the style to the ovule, where it fuses with the female cell. This process is called *fertilization*.

But remember that only pollen from the same species will be "compatible" – able to grow down through the stigma and ovary and fertilize the ovule.

The purpose of flowers is to produce seeds from which a new generation will grow.

Before a seed can form, a flower must be fertilized (see caption to illustration above). But first of all, pollination must take place – pollen must be transferred from the anther (male) to the stigma (female), usually in the flower of another plant.

Different types of pollination
Most flowering plants are *hermaphrodite*, that is they produce both male and female sexual organs in the same flower. So pollen does not have far to travel to reach the female stigma in the same flower. If this happens, it is called *self-pollination*.

However, since the male cell is protected in a pollen grain, it can be transported by wind or by insects over long distances. If pollen reaches the stigma of a flower on another plant, *cross-pollination* will have occurred. The male cell is therefore able to fertilize different plants of the same species – a process called *cross-fertilization*.

In fact, it is far more usual for cross-fertilization to take place, even though most flowers are hermaphrodite. The reasons for this are discussed on page 15.

Pollination

Different methods of pollination

In Europe, flowers are pollinated mainly by *wind* or by *insects*. The same is true in other temperate, Mediterranean and arctic regions of the world. Other animals may sometimes act as pollinators, but this is more common in tropical regions, where birds and bats are important pollinators.

Insect-pollinated flowers are usually colourful, scented and often produce nectar. *Wind-pollinated* flowers tend to be less colourful, often green, with no scent or nectar. Read on for further differences.

Insect-pollination (or entomophilly)

Insect-pollinated flowers usually have a large, colourful, scented corolla (or calyx) which makes them attractive to insects. Insects come to expect some kind of reward when they visit an attractive flower. The reward may be in the form of nectar,

the sweet liquid produced by the nectary, or pollen which is also a nutritious foodstuff for insects. Some flowers such as poppy do not produce nectar and must entice insects by their pollen alone. These flowers produce an abundance of pollen so as to leave some spare for reproductive purposes.

While seeking nectar or collecting pollen from a flower, an insect's body may brush against the stamens and pick up pollen from the anthers. Its pollen-covered body may then contact the stigmas and leave pollen on them.

If the pollen comes from anthers of the same plant then self-pollination will have been carried out. If the pollen came from another plant then cross-pollination will have been achieved.

The pollen

The surface of the entomophillous pollen grain must be sticky or rough in order to adhere to the insect-pollinator's body.

▼ Grasses, like all wind-pollinated flowers, have no need for petals, scent or nectar. Their anthers and stigmas hang outside the flower so pollen is freely released into the wind or picked up from it.

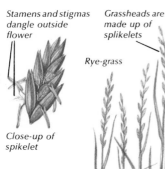

Stamens and stigmas dangle outside flower

Grassheads are made up of splikelets

Rye-grass

Close-up of spikelet

▼ Insect-pollinated flowers have showy petals, and often produce scent and nectar. Some flowers like the poppy have no nectar so must entice insects with their pollen alone. They therefore have lots of stamens to produce abundant pollen.

Colour and pattern

Most insects do not see colours in the same way that people do, but they can see bluish colours as we see them. Because of this, in temperate regions where insects are the chief pollinators to be attracted, a large proportion of flowers are blue.

Insects are also sensitive to ultra-violet rays, invisible to us, which are reflected from the surface of the petals of some flowers. So they see on petals patterns which our eyes cannot detect.

In the tropics, where birds are also important pollinators, there are just as many red flowers as blue ones. This is because birds have the same colour vision as people.

Many petals bear patterns, markings or colour changes, often in ultra-violet wavelengths visible only to insects. These patterns tend to draw the eye towards the centre of the flower. They act as guidelines to the insects, pointing to the nectar and leading the insects into contact with anther and stigma.

▼ Sea bindweed attracts insects with its trumpet-shaped flowers, and then "leads" the insect into the source of nectar with its pink and white stripes. The pink stripes are scented differently from the white stripes too.

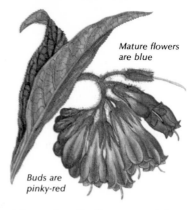

Mature flowers are blue

Buds are pinky-red

▲ In comfrey the flowers are pinky-red in bud and then slowly turn through mauve to blue when they are mature and rich in nectar. Bees are more sensitive to blue than red and will therefore visit the more mature flowers in favour of those which have just opened. The change in colour indicates that they are ready to be pollinated.

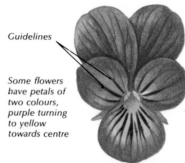

Guidelines

Some flowers have petals of two colours, purple turning to yellow towards centre

▲ The wild pansy "draws" insects inside the flower with its dark stripes.

Flower scents

The overall scent of a flower is in fact the combination of many different scents produced from the surface of the petal. In most flowers the scent changes and becomes stronger towards the base of each petal. Insects therefore have yet another guideline to draw them into the centre of the flower.

Nectar

The nectar of open flowers such as dogrose is contained in shallow pools accessible to any type of insect which visits. But many flowers provide nectar in a reservoir, formed simply by the petals fusing together into a corolla tube.

In some flowers the corolla is extended into spurs, as in toadflax, or pouches, as in snapdragon. Spurs and pouches can contain a large quantity of nectar, and the design of the flower means that only certain insects, for example bees with long tongues, can reach the nectar. This ensures that the correct insect-pollinator visits the flower. The insect, richly rewarded with a large store of nectar, then looks for another flower of the same species. This increases the chances of successful cross-pollination.

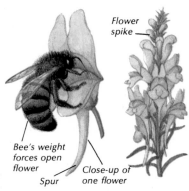

Flower spike

Bee's weight forces open flower

Spur

Close-up of one flower

▲ **Toadflax stores its nectar for the right pollinator by closing the mouth of the corolla. Only the larger bees are heavy enough to open the mouth and obtain the nectar inside the spur – formed of the corolla tube. The nectar is inaccessible to smaller insects whose bodies would be too small to brush against anthers and stigma efficiently.**

▼ **The honeysuckle is pollinated chiefly by moths. It has two devices to attract moths. Firstly, its scent is stronger at night when moths are most active. Secondly, it produces a deep supply of nectar at the end of a long corolla tube, which is only accessible to long-tongued insects.**

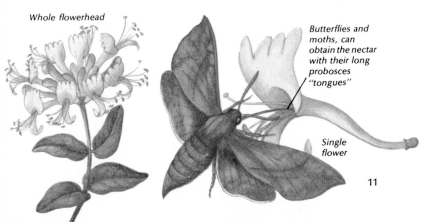

Whole flowerhead

Butterflies and moths, can obtain the nectar with their long proboscis "tongues"

Single flower

Singling out the right pollinator

Primitive flowers (see page 28) such as buttercup and poppy attract, indiscriminately, insects which may have previously visited all kinds of different species. These flowers must produce a large quantity of pollen with their numerous stamens in order to increase the chances of at least some pollen reaching the stigma of the same species. So a lot of pollen is wasted.

The more advanced "closed" flowers can be more economical in their production of pollen since they are designed to attract a single customer. They are pollinated efficiently by one or just a few species of insects which are likely to seek out the same flowers. These more advanced flowers may bear as few as one stamen (see Orchids page 38). The more advanced flowers must have features which prevent pollen or nectar being "stolen" by the wrong species.

Some insects are so tiny that, although they are unable to reach the nectar with their tongues, they may be able to climb down to the nectar source without touching either anther or stigma. Some flowers such as foxglove bar the way to the tiny insects with a battery of hairs. Others such as toadflax shown on page 11 have a closed mouth to the corolla tube. In both cases, only the larger beasts are undeterred and barge their way through, brushing against the anther and stigma.

Teasels prevent ants from reaching ▶ the flowers by catching pools of water in their cupped leaves. Ants are unsuitable as pollinators for most flowers since they are too small and smooth for pollen to stick to their bodies.

▼ The foxglove has a battery of hairs inside its corolla tube. This prevents small insects who would be inefficient pollinators from entering the flower and taking the nectar, since they would get tangled up in the hairs.

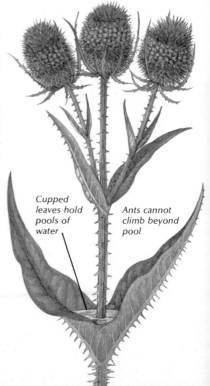

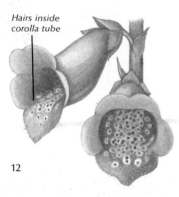

Hairs inside corolla tube

Cupped leaves hold pools of water

Ants cannot climb beyond pool

Wind-pollination (or anemophilly)

Not all flowers are the colourful, showy ones designed to attract insect-pollinators. Flowers which are pollinated by wind have no need for such attractiveness.

Features of wind-pollinated flowers

Wind-pollinated (or anemophillous) flowers are small and inconspicuous and consist mainly of reproductive organs. Grasses, sedges, rushes and most catkin-bearing trees are pollinated by wind. But there are other examples from other families of flowering plants, for instance salad burnet in the rose family, and meadow rue in the buttercup family. In all cases, the inflorescences can be very attractive, but the individual flowers are small and unshowy.

Notice how the anthers are borne on very long filaments and dangle and shake in the wind. A showy display of petals would prevent them moving freely in the wind.

The stigmas of wind-pollinated flowers are usually larger and more feathery than those of insect-pollinated flowers. They are designed to trap pollen grains passing in the wind, unobstructed by a corolla. As in insect-pollinated flowers, only pollen from the same species will be compatible.

The pollen

Anemophillous (wind-borne) pollen grains tend to be smaller and lighter than entomophillous ones. They are therefore more easily transported by slight air currents.

Hazel catkins flower from January to March. All catkins appear early in the year, before the trees' foliage develops and hinders the exchange of pollen in the wind. Like all wind-pollinated flowers, the individual flowers are small and unshowy, though as may be seen here, the inflorescences can be very attractive.

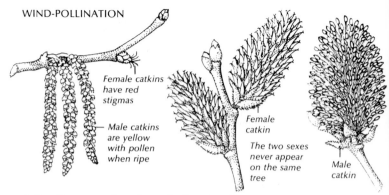

Female catkins have red stigmas

Male catkins are yellow with pollen when ripe

Female catkin

The two sexes never appear on the same tree

Male catkin

▲ Hazel is a monoecious plant – that is one which bears unisexual flowers, either completely male or completely female, on the same plant. Notice how different the male and female catkins are in appearance.

Types of sexuality

Wind-pollinated flowers are often *unisexual* (containing either just male or just female parts) rather than *hermaphrodite* (containing both). Catkin-bearing trees, for example, all have unisexual flowers. The female flowers are gathered into female catkins and the male ones into male catkins.

Sometimes the same plant bears both male and female catkins. Hazel is an example of this.

In other species, for example all the willows, each plant bears either all male or all female catkins.

Hazel then is called *monoecious* (meaning *one* home for both sexes) and willow is called *dioecious* (meaning *two* homes, one for the male and one for the female). Dioecism makes self-pollination impossible, so cross-pollination is necessary if fertilization is to take place. Cross-pollination is more common anyway, whether a plant is unisexual or hermaphrodite (see pages 15–18).

▲ Willows are dioecious plants – meaning that each plant bears either all male or all female flowers. Willow catkins are pollinated both by wind and by insects, since, though there is no showy corolla, willow catkins do produce nectar.

The world distribution of wind- and insect-pollinated plants

Flowering plants are thought to have originated in tropical climates. In the humid atmosphere of the tropical rain forest there are few breezes let alone wind, so most flowers are pollinated by insects and birds.

In contrast, in the more severe regions of the world – in the arctic and in areas at high altitude – the plants that can survive are mainly wind-pollinated. It would seem therefore that these plants have adapted to these grim regions by developing features to cope with the conditions. Since there are comparatively few insects around, but an unlimited supply of relentless wind, flowers have evolved features to use the wind to pollinate them.

Wind-pollinated flowers are therefore thought to have evolved from insect-pollinated ones, spreading outwards from the tropics where flowering plants are most likely to have originated.

Self- versus cross-pollination

Most flowers are capable of self-pollination, since they contain both male and female parts. However, though self-fertilization is not harmful, if it takes place repeatedly over a few generations of plants, it may not do the species much good (but see page 18 and also "Wasteland weeds" pages 42–43).

Disadvantages of self-fertilization
Seeds produced by self-fertilization (that is fusion between male and female sex cells from the *same* plant) will grow into offspring which are almost identical to the parent plant.

The new generation will probably be ideally suited to the habitat in which the parent is growing. But there will not be much variation amongst all the different offspring, and they will therefore be less adaptable to new places or to the parent's habitat if it should change a great deal.

Another possible disadvantage of self-fertilization is that undesirable characteristics may be passed on to the next generation. If self-fertilization takes place repeatedly over a few generations, these characteristics may become exaggerated.

Advantages of cross-fertilization
If cross-fertilization takes place (that is the fusion of male and female sex cells from *different* plants), the offspring produced will have a number of characteristics different from either of the parents. So at least some of them will be more likely to conquer new places, or even different types of habitat, or survive in the parents' habitat if it should alter.

Because of the disadvantages of self-fertilization, most plants have features to favour cross-fertilization.

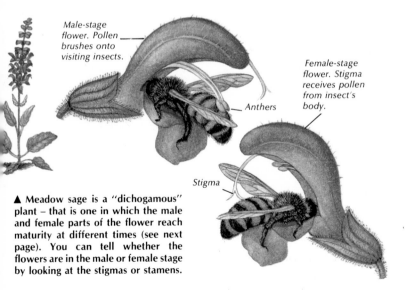

Male-stage flower. Pollen brushes onto visiting insects.

Female-stage flower. Stigma receives pollen from insect's body.

Anthers

Stigma

▲ Meadow sage is a "dichogamous" plant – that is one in which the male and female parts of the flower reach maturity at different times (see next page). You can tell whether the flowers are in the male or female stage by looking at the stigmas or stamens.

Staggered development

Self-pollination is less likely to occur when the male and female parts of the flower reach maturity at different times. This is called "dichogamy", and plants in which this happens are said to be "dichogamous". Either the stigma becomes receptive to pollen only after the pollen-bearing anthers have withered; or the stigma may mature before the stamens and anthers. Therefore pollination will result only if pollen has been received from another flower. The flower will generally be on another plant, so cross-pollination results.

Dichogamy, however does not entirely eliminate the risk of self-pollination. Rosebay willowherb is a common example of a dichogamous plant. Like many other species, this plant has a raceme of several flowers, which open in sequence over several weeks. This means that flowers on the same plant will be at different stages of maturity. Pollen could easily pass from a "male-stage" flower to a "female-stage" flower on the same plant, risking in-breeding.

In fact, self-pollination seldom occurs because the flowers open from the bottom of the plant upwards. Bees tend to visit the lowermost flowers first, and work their way up the plant. So they will visit the more mature (female-stage) flowers first, and the pollen-bearing (male-stage) flowers afterwards.

Rosebay willowherb is another ▶ "dichogamous" plant. The more mature flowers in the female stage tend to be lower down the plant, and bees will visit these first. So pollen is likely to be transferred to *another* plant.

Flowers of different sexes on the same plant

Another way in which plants may restrict self-fertilization is by monoecism. A monoecious plant produces two types of flowers – male flowers which develop only stamens, and female flowers in which ovaries develop but no stamens. Many trees, for example birch and hazel (see page 14), are monoecious.

But, like the dichogamous rosebay willowherb, pollen can still be transferred from one flower to another on the same plant, but the chances of self-pollination occurring are reduced.

Male-stage flower – ripe stamens, stigma not yet forked

Female-stage flower – anthers withered, stigma forked ready to receive pollen

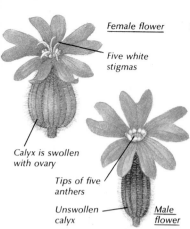

Female flower

Five white stigmas

Calyx is swollen with ovary

Tips of five anthers

Unswollen calyx

Male flower

▲ Red campion is a "dioecious" plant, each plant producing either all male or all female flowers. Look for stigmas or stamens, or squeeze the calyx gently, to find out whether a flower is male or female.

Flowers of one sex only on each plant
Certain species avoid self-pollination in another way: each plant bears either all female or all male flowers. This is called "dioecism". Many plants of the Silene genus (campions and catchflies) and many trees, such as the willows, are dioecious (see page 14).

It is easy to tell if the flower of a dioecious plant, such as red campion, is male or female. Look into the mouth of the corolla to see if stamens or stigmas are emerging. Or squeeze the calyx gently to see if you can feel a swelling – this will be the fruit developing from a fertilized ovary of a female flower.

The problem with dioecism is that, though it ensures cross-pollination, it makes self-pollination impossible. So if during bad weather insect-pollinators are scarce, no seed may be set at all. Some species which are dioecious in mild climates, are only partly dioecious in severe climates.

For instance, moss campion, which grows on mountains and sea cliffs, is dioecious in the Pyrenees. In the Arctic, however, many plants of this species bear hermaphrodite (male and female) flowers. In Britain, with its relatively mild climate, the species is not completely dioecious, but fewer plants bear hermaphrodite flowers than they do in the Arctic.

Stigmas which prevent self-pollination
Some plants can prevent self-fertilization altogether by producing pollen which is not compatible with the stigmas of the same plant, in the same way that pollen and stigmas are incompatible between different plant species. So only pollen from another plant (of the same species) is able to penetrate the ovary wall. This feature is called *self-incompatibility*.

Some species which have this feature show outward signs of it. For instance the primrose produces two types of plants – one with "pin-eyed" flowers and one with

▼ The primrose prevents self-pollination by producing two types of plants – one with pin-eyed and one with thrum-eyed flowers. The pollen of one type is not compatible with the other type.

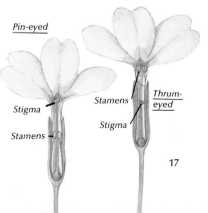

Pin-eyed

Thrum-eyed

Stamens

Stigma

Stigma

Stamens

"thrum-eyed" flowers. Pollen from a pin-eyed plant is incompatible not only with its own stigma but also with the stigmas of all other pin-eyed plants, and vice-versa with thrum-eyed plants. So cross-pollination, from pin-eyed to thrum-eyed flowers or vice-versa, is ensured. You can see the difference between the two types by looking at the flower centres (see page 17). Look at a bank of primroses and try to work out the proportion of each type – there should be about half and half.

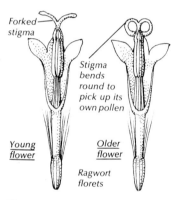

Forked stigma

Stigma bends round to pick up its own pollen

Young flower

Older flower

Ragwort florets

Self-pollination as a preference or as a last resort

Some species have features to ensure self-pollination if cross-pollination has not taken place towards the end of the flowering period. Examples of this include violets, honeysuckle and members of the daisy family (Compositae).

Other species can produce seeds without fertilization taking place at all. This is called *apomyxis*. Offspring are identical to the parent plant, so in this way apomyxis is similar to vegetative reproduction (see page 26).

Both these types of plants may risk the disadvantages of self-pollination if it is repeated over several generations. But reproduction is at least ensured, and in some cases this is more important than producing variations in the offspring (see "Wasteland weeds" pages 42–43).

◀ Towards the end of their flowering period, daisy flowers make sure that self-pollination takes place if cross-pollination has failed: the stigma bends down to pick up pollen from the anthers of the same flowers.

▼ Honeysuckle flowers can be seen towards the end of the flowering period with their stigma drooping down, to pick up their own pollen.

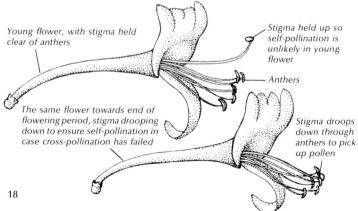

Young flower, with stigma held clear of anthers

Stigma held up so self-pollination is unlikely in young flower

Anthers

The same flower towards end of flowering period, stigma drooping down to ensure self-pollination in case cross-pollination has failed

Stigma droops down through anthers to pick up pollen

Fruits and seeds

From flower to fruit (in poppy)

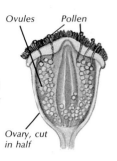

Stigma

Ovary

Ovules   *Pollen*

Ovary, cut in half

1. Pollination: Pollen from one flower is left on the stigma of another by a visiting bee.

2. The male cell emerges from the pollen grain and grows down inside the ovary, which contains many ovules.

3. Fertilization: On reaching an ovule, the male cell fuses with the female cell of the ovule.

6. Seed dispersal: When the fruit ripens, holes form in the top, so when the fruit is shaken in the wind, seeds fall out and are blown away from the parent plant.

4. The fertilized ovules begin to develop into seeds. The petals and stamens die and fall.

5. The ovaries swell and develop into a fruit containing the seeds.

The purpose of flowers and fruits

At the end of the flowering season, the plant world becomes festooned with a mass of fruits of different shapes, sizes, colours and textures. They have all developed from successful flowers.

The **purpose of flowers** is to produce seeds from fertilized ovules in the ovary. The petals start to wither, since they have finished their task of attracting insect-pollinators. At the same time the ovary wall begins to develop into a fruit.

The **purpose of fruits**, whatever their structure, is to ensure that seeds are dispersed – distributed away from the parent plant. This gives the seedlings a chance to develop without too much competition from other plants of the same species.

Different methods of seed dispersal

Seeds may be carried to different places in a variety of ways, but the commonest methods are by *wind*, by *animals* (either on their fur or through their droppings), by *explosion* of the fruit, or, in the case of many aquatic plants, by *water*.

By wind. Many plants bear fruits with features which enable them to become airborne.

By animals. Succulent fruits may be eaten by animals. The seeds are not digested but pass out in the droppings.
  Some fruits have hooks or prickles so that they catch on to the coats of passing animals, and drop off later onto "new" soil.

By explosion. Some fruits explode when ripe so the seeds inside are scattered away from the parent plant.

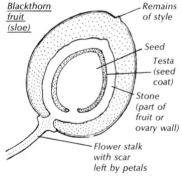

Different types of fruits

The fruits that first spring to mind are *succulent* (juicy) fruits like oranges and plums. The different forms of succulent fruits are shown below and opposite. Overleaf the various types of *dry* fruits, like acorns and pea pods, are described.

Succulent fruits

The sweet juicy flesh of succulent fruits is an important source of food for animals, especially birds. Often the whole fruit is eaten – seeds and all. The seeds are not digested and are passed out in the animals' droppings, often quite far away from the parent plant. Some seeds cannot germinate unless they are first activated by an animal's digestive juices.

Drupes ▶
The fruit (called a sloe) of the blackthorn bush has a hard centre or stone which contains the seed. The fruit develops from a flower which blossomed several months before. The flower had a *single ovary* containing just one ovule or seed. This type of fruit is called a *drupe*.

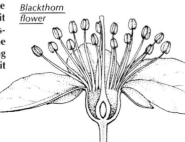

Blackthorn fruit (sloe)

Remains of style

Seed

Testa (seed coat)

Stone (part of fruit or ovary wall)

Flower stalk with scar left by petals

Blackthorn flower

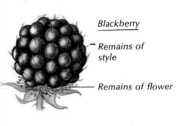

Blackberry

Remains of style

Remains of flower

Remains of flower

Fleshy receptacle

Seed (ovule)

Flower stalk

<u>Rosehip</u>

Core – ovary with seeds

Fleshy receptacle

Remains of flower

<u>Apple</u>

Seed (pip)

Flower stalk

Core – ovary with seeds

Drupules ▲

The blackberry fruit of bramble bushes consists of a collection of drupes called *drupules*. Each drupule is similar in structure to the blackthorn sloe. If you look closely at a blackberry, especially an unripe one, you can still see the remains of the style attached to the top of each ovary. If you compare this to a flower which is still in bloom, you can, with the aid of a magnifying glass, see the tiny ovaries waiting to be pollinated. Once fertilized, they will swell up into succulent drupules.

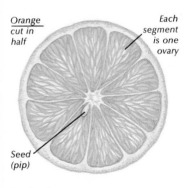

<u>Orange cut in half</u>

Each segment is one ovary

Seed (pip)

Berries ▲

The succulent fruits of orange trees and tomato plants are technically called *berries*. This is because they are made up of *more than one ovary fused together*. (In bramble for instance the ovaries are not fused to each other.) In the orange, illustrated above, each segment is formed from one of the ovaries making up the whole fruit.

False fruits ▲

Rosehips and apples are not like drupes and berries. This is because the true fruit is in fact the core, which consists of the ovaries. The whole is called a false fruit because the fleshy part is not part of the ovary: it is the swollen top of the flower stalk – the receptacle. The fleshy portion has enveloped the true fruit.

21

Dry fruits

There are two ways in which dry fruits help seeds to be scattered. Either the whole fruit is formed with features to aid dispersal, or else it bursts open while still attached to the plant, so the seeds are catapulted clear of their parent. Fruits which burst open are called *dehiscent* fruits. Those which do not burst open are called *indehiscent*.

▲ The broom pod twists as it splits violently open, catapulting the seeds away.

Dehiscent fruits

If you sit near a gorse bush or amongst a patch of campions in summer you can hear little snapping sounds as the fruits of these plants split open. Any seeds that remain inside the fruit will be tossed clear when the wind blows and shakes the dry stalks.

Dehiscent fruits may be in the form of *legumes* (or *pods*), which are formed from single ovaries; or *capsules* which, like berries, are fruits made up of a number of ovaries fused together.

▼ The fruit of shepherd's purse, like other members of the cabbage family (Cruciferae), is made up of ovaries which pull apart when the seeds are ready for dispersal.

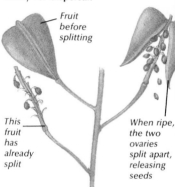

Fruit before splitting

This fruit has already split

When ripe, the two ovaries split apart, releasing seeds

▼ **Campion capsules, when ripe and dry, split open at the top to release the seeds.**

▼ **The poppy capsule forms holes at the top when ripe, like a pepperpot.**

Seeds are shaken out through holes (pores) when wind blows

▼ Cranesbill in fruit. The styles are fused together before the fruit is fully ripe. When it is ripe, the styles split apart rapidly and peel away upwards, flinging the single-seeded ovaries away.

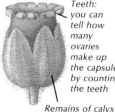

Teeth: you can tell how many ovaries make up the capsule by counting the teeth

Remains of calyx (sepals)

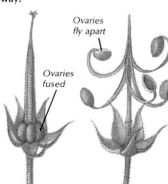

Ovaries fly apart

Ovaries fused

Indehiscent fruits

These fruits must get clear of the parent plant before the fruit wall rots and releases the seeds.

In some the seeds are so rich in food that animals will collect them and carry them off, in the same way as they do succulent fruits. This type of indehiscent fruit includes nuts such as acorns and chestnuts.

In others the ovary wall develops a rough or prickly surface, which gets caught in the fur of passing animals. Later, when the animal cleans its coat, these *burrs* are pushed off onto "new" soil.

Many indehiscent fruits have special features like wings or parachutes which enable them to be carried on the wind.

Dandelion "clock"

Each fruit has a stalk with a "parachute"

Try shaking a thistle head to see how far each parachute travels before falling to the ground

Single fruit (enlarged)

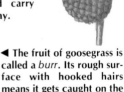

▶ The acorn nut is rich in food-stuff for animals, who collect the nuts and carry them away.

◀ The fruit of goosegrass is called a *burr*. Its rough surface with hooked hairs means it gets caught on the coats of passing animals and is carried away.

▼ The fruit wall may be expanded into a wing, as it is in ash keys below and also in maple. The wings enable the fruits to flutter away in the wind.

Winged fruit of ash

▲ Dandelion clocks and thistle down are a familiar sight. Both species belong to the daisy family (Compositae), and many plants in this family produce fruits equipped with parachutes.

In late summer notice how often the air is filled with clouds of thistle down. A few of the fruits travel enormous distances from the parent plant, but many do not get far.

Try shaking out into the wind the fruits of one thistle head to see how far each parachute travels before falling to the ground. Only those seeds which land on bare ground will be able to grow. Try and estimate the average percentage of successfully dispersed seeds in one thistle head.

23

Growth and food production

From seed to seedling (in sunflower)

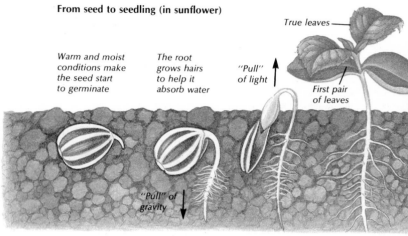

True leaves

Warm and moist conditions make the seed start to germinate

The root grows hairs to help it absorb water

"Pull" of light

First pair of leaves

"Pull" of gravity

1. At *germination*, the outer coat (testa) splits and the seedling begins to emerge.

2. Part of it becomes the root, growing downwards, guided by the force of gravity.

3. The part which becomes the shoot grows towards the light. The shoot soon grows leaves.

4. Once the leaves develop, they use energy from sunlight to make food (see below).

What makes a seed germinate?

A seed will germinate once it finds itself in a suitable habitat and once the temperature and moistness of the soil are right. The seeds of some plants require a trigger to "break their dormancy" – to stimulate them into germination. They may need to undergo something quite violent such as freezing weather or being eaten by a bird, whose digestive juices break the seed's dormancy.

Using sunlight to make food

A plant can obtain some of the nutrients it needs from the soil by absorbing them along with water through the roots. The main nutrients which can be absorbed in this way are nitrates, phosphates and potassium.

But a plant *must* also have sugars and starch which it cannot get from the soil. All green plants can use their leaves to manufacture sugars by an amazing process called *photosynthesis*. The green pigment in plants is called *chlorophyll* and this is the only substance on earth which can harness energy from *sunlight*. The energy can then be used to combine carbon dioxide and water and build energy-rich sugars and starches from them. These sugars and starches form the basis of food for all animals including humans. Oxygen, so important to animals, is given off as a by-product of photosynthesis. Without green plants, life on earth as we know it would be impossible.

Storing food

Plants often produce more sugars and starch than they need. Many can store this extra during the periods when they stop growing such as in cold times or in times of drought. The food can then be used when the plant begins to grow again and produce a new crop of leaves and/or flowers. Plants which can store food, and can therefore live for several years, are called *perennials*.

The plants which do not put by a food store, but which die within the year, after flowering and setting seed, are called *annuals*. Annuals therefore rely on their seeds germinating successfully each year in order for the species to survive. Perennials are not as dependent on this, since they will live on through the next growing season, and will have another chance to produce seeds.

Ways of storing food
Perennial plants may have one of several types of storage organs, which are "modified" stems, leaves or roots. Here are some examples.

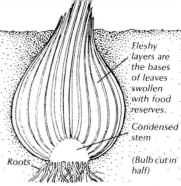

Fleshy layers are the bases of leaves swollen with food reserves.

Condensed stem

Roots

(Bulb cut in half)

▲ *Bulbs*: **The daffodil stores food in a bulb, which consists of the bases of leaves swollen with food and a very short stem, and roots. Like many bulb-producing species, it can produce flowers early in the year by using its mass of stored food.**

Food-storing roots: ▶
The carrot, for example, has a tap root swollen with stored food.

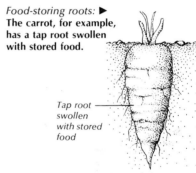

Tap root swollen with stored food

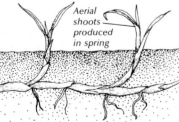

Aerial shoots produced in spring

▲ *Rhizome*: **Some plants such as grasses store food during winter in a horizontal underground stem called a rhizome.**
Corms: Corms, such as the crocus corm, are squat underground stems which store food. Each year a new corm forms on top of the old one, which shrivels up.

▼ *Tuber*: The potato plant stores food in a tuber which is in fact the swollen tip of a rhizome.

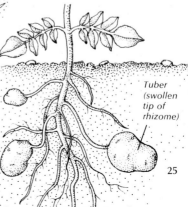

Tuber (swollen tip of rhizome)

Vegetative reproduction

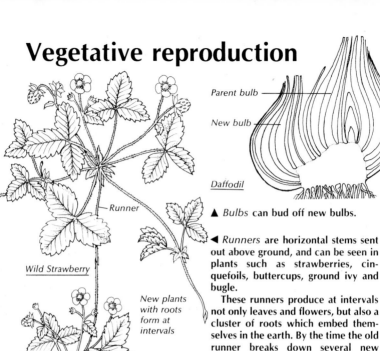

Parent bulb

New bulb

Daffodil

▲ *Bulbs* can bud off new bulbs.

Runner

Wild Strawberry

New plants with roots form at intervals

◀ *Runners* are horizontal stems sent out above ground, and can be seen in plants such as strawberries, cinquefoils, buttercups, ground ivy and bugle.

These runners produce at intervals not only leaves and flowers, but also a cluster of roots which embed themselves in the earth. By the time the old runner breaks down several new plants have become established.

If plants experience bad weather during crucial stages of their life cycle they may not be able to reproduce by means of flowers and seeds. Cold weather, high wind or rain may prevent flowers from developing, insect-pollinators from taking to the wing, or seeds from germinating.

So some plants, especially in regions with unpredictable weather, rely on other methods to reproduce. These methods usually involve a portion of the parent plant breaking off and growing into a new plant. This process is called *vegetative reproduction*.

One important but little observed method is when sections of a *rhizome* system disintegrate, leaving several separate plants. *Bulbs* bud

off new bulbs. *Tubers* separate from rhizomes and grow into new plants. Many *water plants* can reproduce vegetatively: a branch or twig broken from a willow may float downstream, lodge in a bank and sprout into a new tree. Some plants can send out *runners* (see illustration above).

Even though vegetative reproduction is very successful and often more reliable than sexual reproduction, it has two disadvantages. Firstly, only a few new plants are formed, whereas hundreds of seedlings can form as a result of sexual reproduction. Secondly, it means that all the offspring are identical to the parent, which is not always a good thing (see pages 15–18).

How flowering plants evolved

Flowering plants are the most advanced and highly evolved group of plants, as you can see from the illustrations below.

The evolutionary stages in the animal kingdom are generally better known than those of plants. Simple sea creatures were the first to evolve, followed by reptiles including dinosaurs. When the dinosaurs and other giant reptiles disap-peared, birds and mammals became more and more widespread and diverse.

The earliest plants also lived in water. About 400 million years ago new forms like mosses evolved and grew on land. Plants developed flowers at about the same time as true birds evolved and replaced the huge pterodactyls and toothed birds, about 65 million years ago.

Stages of evolution in plants

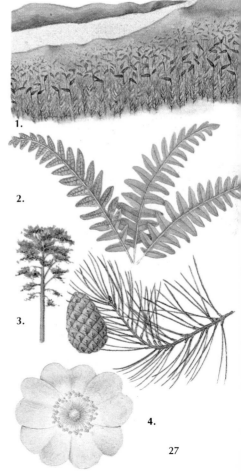

1. *Mosses* and *liverworts* have evolved from some of the earliest land plants. They can only grow when they are very damp, and, having no roots, absorb moisture all over their surface. They reproduce by spores which must fall in wet places in order to form new plants.

2. *Club mosses* and *ferns* developed roots, leaves and a system of veins to transport water from the roots to the rest of the plant. They could therefore grow taller and live in less damp places than the mosses and liverworts, but are still dependent on spores, and there-fore on water, for reproduction.

3. *Conifers* produced large, strong complex seeds instead of tiny spores. The seedling needs moisture to grow but not nearly as much as spores do. Conifers could therefore grow away from damp habitats, and being strong and woody, they became very tall and dominant. But their seeds are not well protected in the cone.

4. *Flowering plants* took this system of reproduction a stage further by enclosing and so protecting the seed in an ovary.

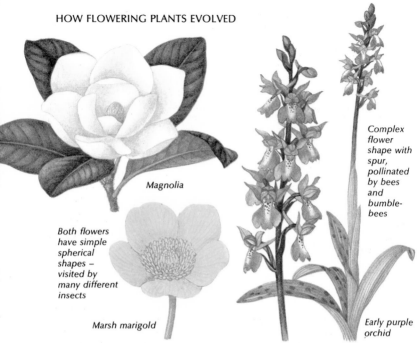

Magnolia

Complex flower shape with spur, pollinated by bees and bumble-bees

Both flowers have simple spherical shapes – visited by many different insects

Marsh marigold

Early purple orchid

▲ The magnolia and the marsh marigold are both primitively designed flowers. Notice their simple shapes and large numbers of stamens and ovaries. All kinds of insect-pollinators visit these flowers, so a large amount of pollen must be produced.

▲ One of the most advanced and highly evolved families of flowers in the world is the orchids. Orchids, like many other advanced flowers, single out certain insects to carry out pollination. They do this so efficiently that they need only one stamen. See also pages 38–39.

The evolution of the flower

One of the most primitively designed flowers still living today is the magnolia. In Britain one of our most primitive native flowers is the marsh marigold.

Evolution did not stop once the flower was produced. The flower produced more and more efficient methods of carrying out pollination, and the designs of the flowers became adapted to suit different pollinators, leading to the wonderful range of flowers we see today.

Adaptation in flowering plants

Furthermore, flowering plants continued (and still continue) to adapt themselves to survive in harsher and harsher situations, by developing features that enable them to cope with difficult conditions. They are now found in every situation on earth, even in deserts.

You can see some of the ways in which flowering plants have adapted in the following two parts of this book.

FLOWER FAMILIES
How plants are grouped

As you get to know more about flowers, it will be useful to look for similarities in the shape of the flower, and the number of parts, since it is the design alone which indicates that one flower may be related to another – and thus belong to the same family, or group.

Buttercups – a primitive family
Buttercups, crowfoots and pasque flowers, even though not of the same colour, all belong to the same family – the Ranunculaceae. Members of this family tend to have round flowers with petals of even lengths, and numerous stamens and ovaries. This is a primitive design which does not single out a particular type of insect for pollination, and must therefore produce a large quantity of pollen (see page 9).

▼ **All these flowers belong to the buttercup family. They all have lots of stamens, and petals of even length, giving the whole flower a roundish shape.**

Labiate flowers – an advanced family
Common examples of the Labiate family are yellow archangel, red dead-nettle, catmint and self-heal. In each the petals are fused together to form a long narrow corolla tube which contains the nectar. This design singles out the long-tongued insects to carry out pollination.

These flowers also provide a platform for the insect to land on, and the stamens and style arch over to touch the visiting insect's back. There are several other flowers which have this advanced design, so all are grouped together into one family – the Labiatae, illustrated overleaf.

Bulbous buttercup

Pasque flower

Pheasant's eye

Wood anemone

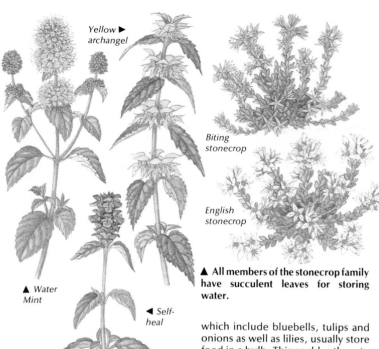

Yellow ► archangel

Biting stonecrop

English stonecrop

▲ Water Mint

◄ Self-heal

▲ All members of the stonecrop family have succulent leaves for storing water.

▲ Some species in the Labiate family – note the "lipped" fused petals and leaves in opposite pairs.

Other family characteristics

It is the flower of a plant which determines which family it belongs to. But members of a family often have other features in common, just because they are related.

For example, all members of the Labiate family have leaves arranged in opposite pairs, and they are also often aromatic: mints, thymes and sage are all Labiates.

The stonecrop family (Crassulaceae) has many species with succulent leaves for storing water – a useful feature in dry habitats. Members of the lily family (Liliaceae), which include bluebells, tulips and onions as well as lilies, usually store food in a bulb. This enables them to make an early start in the spring, which is very important in habitats where the summertime is not suitable for growth, so that the life cycle must be completed very early in the year.

Once you know the basic characteristics of some widespread families (see pages 31–34), you will find it much easier to identify them quickly when using a field guide in which the species are arranged in family order.

Sub-grouping in families

Most families contain so many species that they have been organized into sub-groups. These are called *genera* (*genus* is the singular form of the word). For example, *Anemone* is a genus in the buttercup family and *Mentha* (mints) is a genus in the Labiate family.

The top 20 families

When you are trying to identify an unfamiliar flower, it is fairly daunting to know that it could be any one of thousands. There are over 11,000 species in Europe, and about 1,500 of these are found in Britain.

Most identification guides show the flowers arranged in family order. So if you can recognize the family of a flower, it will save hunting through the entire book to identify it.

The "top 20"

Although there are 173 families of flowering plants represented in Europe (about 122 families in Britain), it is encouraging to know that more than three–quarters of them belong to only twenty families. So if you are able to recognize the characteristics of these top twenty, you will have found a short cut to identifying flowers.

The following notes show the main family features which will help you identify its members. The families are split into four groups. The first three – the *Dicotyledons* – contain plants with net-veined leaves (as in red campion). In the fourth group – the Mono-cotyledons – the leaf veins run *parallel* to the length of the leaf (as in tulip). The first group has small unshowy flowers, the second has petals that are *not* fused together, and the third has fused petals.

How to use the "top 20" notes

When you find an unfamiliar flower, first decide to which group it belongs (see above). All the families of flowering plants belong to one of these groups but only the top twenty families are listed on pages 32–34.

Next decide whether or not you think the plant belongs to one of these top twenty. If you think it does, turn to the pages showing the particular family in an identification book or field guide and look through for the best match. The more you use an identification book, the more you will come to recognize the characteristics which hold each family together.

If your unfamiliar plant does not seem to fit into any of the top twenty, it will be one from the other 153 families. You will find you already know something about a few of them such as the willowherbs, heathers and violets.

▼ An unfamiliar European flower could be any one of over 11,000 species. But by using the notes on pages 32–34 you will get to know the main features of the twenty most common families, and this will give you a short cut to identification.

Group 1: Families with net-veined leaves and insignificant flowers (though inflorescences may be showy).

1. Willow family: Salicaceae ▼
Flowers are borne in unisexual catkins, either all male or all female on each plant. Plants are trees or shrubs. Species difficult to tell apart.

▼ 2. Dock and bistort family: Polygonaceae   **3. Goosefoot family: Chenopodiaceae ▼**
Both easily recognized as families, but species difficult to tell apart.

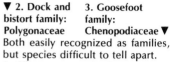

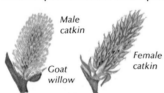

Male catkin

Goat willow

Female catkin

Common sorrel

Fat hen

Group 2: Families with net-veined leaves and unfused petals.

4. Pink family: Caryophyllaceae ▼
Petals are often cleft. Most species have five petals, some have four. Leaves in opposite pairs. Inflorescences often branched cymes.

5. Buttercup family: Ranunculaceae ▼
All flowers (except very few) have round flowers, petals of even length and numerous stamens. No epicalyx as seen in Rose family.

Bladder campion

Maiden pink

Monks-hood

Meadow buttercup

6. Cabbage family: Cruciferae ▼
Flowers of all species have four widely-separated petals and usually six stamens. Many species have a raceme of small flowers. Not easily confused with Poppy family.

7. Rose family: Rosaceae ▼
All species have round flowers with petals of even lengths. Most have an epicalyx – an extra ring of sepals. Herbs, shrubs and trees.

(Poppies have four overlapping petals)

Charlock

Dogrose

Epicalyx — seen from below

Cinquefoil

8. Pea family: Leguminosae ▼ – Design of flowers unique – one upper standard petal, two wings and a keel. See also pages 35–36.

9. Cow parsley family: Umbelliferae ▼
Easily recognized as a family, usually with compound umbel inflorescence, but species hard to tell apart.

Restharrow

Hogweed

Group 3: Flowers with net-veined leaves and fused petals.

10. Primrose family: Primulaceae ▼
Round flowers with five petals of even length. Inflorescence often an umbel.

Primrose   Umbel   Scarlet pimpernel

11. Gentian family: Gentianaceae ▼
Round flowers with five petals of even length. Inflorescence usually a branched cyme. Leaves in opposite pairs.

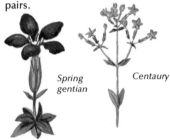

Spring gentian   Centaury

12. Forget-me-not family: Boraginaceae ▼
Round flowers with petals of even length (except for viper's bugloss), and five stamens. Often petals change colour from red (or yellow) to blue. Often inflorescence is a coiled cyme. Leaves are arranged alternately on the stem.

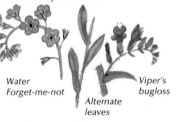

Water Forget-me-not   Alternate leaves   Viper's bugloss

13. Labiate family: Labiatae ▼
All flowers have two lips (except for bugle which has no top lip) and four stamens. Stems always square in cross-section, and leaves in opposite pairs.

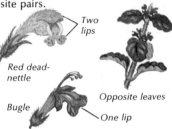

Two lips

Red dead-nettle

Opposite leaves

Bugle   One lip

14. Figwort family: Scrophulariaceae ▼
Very varied designs in flowers. For more information see page 37.

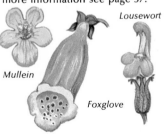

Mullein   Lousewort   Foxglove

15. Daisy family: Compositae ▼
Inflorescence a capitulum of tiny flowers (see page 6). Many species have parachuted fruits.

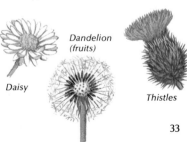

Daisy   Dandelion (fruits)   Thistles

Group 4: Families with parallel-veined leaves.

16. Lily family: Liliaceae ▼
The three petals and three sepals look similar. Six stamens. Many have bulbs.

Lily-of-the-valley

Chives

17. Orchid family: Orchidaceae ▼
Shapes of flowers rather varied, but always have prominent, sometimes multi-coloured, lower lips; often with spur. Only one stamen. See pages 38–39 for more information.

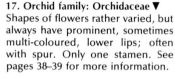

Lip

Marsh helleborine

Lip

Bee orchid

18. Rush family: Juncaceae ▼
Tiny flowers with chaffy petals. Wind-pollinated. Narrow cylindrical leaves, hollow inside, or grass-like leaves with silky hairs.

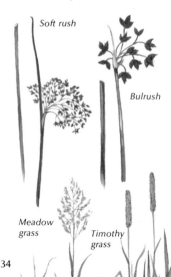

Soft rush

Bulrush

Meadow grass

Timothy grass

19. Sedge family: Cyperaceae ▼
Stems are triangular across, and the leaves are stiff. Flowers of different sexes usually in separate spikes on same stem. Wind-pollinated.

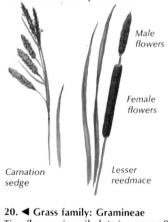

Male flowers

Female flowers

Carnation sedge

Lesser reedmace

20. ◀ Grass family: Gramineae
Tiny flowers in spikelets (see page 9) arranged in spikes or racemes.

The pea family

Surviving in poor soils

The pea family (Leguminosae) – see page 32, no. 8 – is one of the most important in the world: all its members are able to feed on nitrogen in the air. Nitrogen is one of the most essential plant nutrients. Most plants obtain it from the soil, where nitrates are dissolved in water. Soils in many places are very poor in nitrates, but the air, some of which finds its way into the soil, contains 80 per cent nitrogen. This is useless to most plants, but members of the pea family can absorb it. They do so by means of bacteria which live in lumps (nodules) in their roots. It is these bacteria which absorb the nitrogen and give it to the plant in return for sugars and a place to live. This kind of partnership, in which both organisms benefit from each other, is called *symbiosis*.

When a plant's leaves fall, and when it eventually dies, the nitrogen it accumulated is put into the soil. So pea species *improve* the nutrient level of the soil.

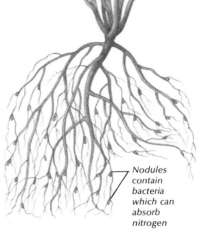

Nodules contain bacteria which can absorb nitrogen

▲ **Root system of a member of the pea family, showing nodules.**

The leaves

The leaves of the pea family are mostly compound – divided up into a number of smaller leaflets either in opposite pairs as in vetches or in groups of three as in laburnum and clovers. Many species have tendrils at the tip of the leaves, to help them scramble over other vegetation to reach the light.

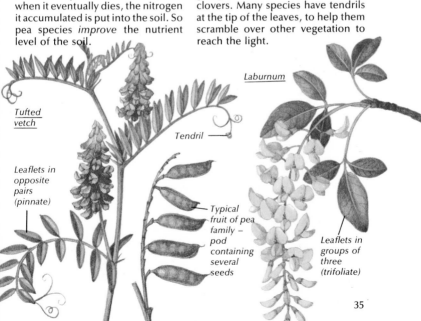

Laburnum

Tufted vetch

Tendril

Leaflets in opposite pairs (pinnate)

Typical fruit of pea family – pod containing several seeds

Leaflets in groups of three (trifoliate)

THE PEA FAMILY

Flower design and pollination

At first glance a clover plant and a broom shrub do not seem to have much in common. But compare the flowers of each, shown on this page, and you will see why both are members of the pea family.

In fact all European species in this family have flowers with petals in the form of a keel, two wings and a standard. So they are all pollinated in a similar way to the broom shown below. The size of the pollinating insects varies according to the size of the flower. But, in order to obtain food – pollen or nectar – from any pea species, an insect must depress the keel, releasing the style and stamens.

Pollination in broom flowers

1. The stamens and style of a broom flower are held within the *keel*, which is flanked by two wings, with the largest petal, called a standard, upright above.

2. A bee in search of pollen (broom contains no nectar) lands on the wings of the flower. The bee's weight pushes the wings down along with the keel which bursts open immediately. The style and some of the stamens swing up and over, hitting the bee's back. So the stigma picks up pollen from other flowers which has stuck to the bee's

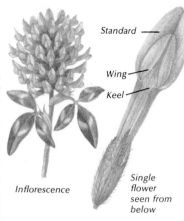

Standard
Wing
Keel

Inflorescence

Single flower seen from below

▲ **If you look at a single flower in the cluster of red clover flowers, you will see its pea-like features. Like the broom below, it has a standard petal, two wings and a keel.**

body, and the stamens leave their pollen on it. The bee can eat pollen left on its belly by shorter stamens, so it is enticed to carry on visiting broom flowers.

3. Once an insect has "opened" a broom flower, the keel stays down and the stamens and style cannot return to their original position. This means that the stigma cannot be pollinated if pollination fails at the first visit of a bee. But in most other members of the pea family, several visits can be made by pollinating insects.

(Broom flowers)

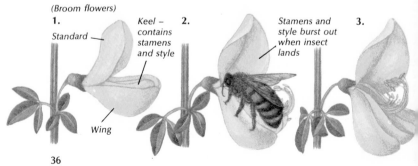

1.
Standard
Keel – contains stamens and style
Wing

2.
Stamens and style burst out when insect lands

3.

The figwort family

The figwort family (Scrophulariaceae) – see page 33, no. 14 – contains some flowers with very curious designs and some with simple shapes. Unlike most families, it is difficult to see what links them together.

But two aspects of the family can be seen quite clearly to have evolved in a very interesting way. Firstly, the designs of the flowers themselves have become more and more complicated and highly adapted: for example compare mullein to foxglove and finally to toadflax, (see pages 11 and 33).

Secondly, some of the more highly evolved plants within the family are semi-parasites. Few species of *flowering* plants are parasites. Plant parasites do not manufacture all their own sugars and starch by photosynthesis as non-parasitic plants do. Instead they sponge off other plants (their *hosts*) for some or all their nourishment. Most are particular about which host species they feed off. Grasses and members of the pea family are favourite hosts since they can flourish even on poor soils. This means that semi-parasites too can live on poor soils – but only by cheating, sponging off others.

Most of the figwort family are normal non-parasitic plants, but a number are semi-parasitic.

Some of the semi-parasites in ▶ the figwort family have very attractive flowers, such as the eyebright and yellow rattle illustrated here, and the lousewort shown on page 47. All three feed off grasses for extra nourishment. But you can tell from their small green leaves that they *do* photosynthesize a little as well.

No green leaves

Notice how similar the flowers are to those of eyebright below

The parasitic ▶ broomrapes have no green leaves with which to photosynthesize. They used to be included in the figwort family, representing the final stage in the trend towards parasitism. But since broomrapes are total parasites, they have now been given a family of their own, called Orobanchaceae.

Eyebright, a tiny flower mainly found on chalk and limestone

Yellow rattle – when in fruit its dry capsule rattles with seeds when the wind blows

The orchid family

Orchids (see page 34, no. 17) have always been one of the most popular families among flower-lovers. Many of its species are nearing extinction because of over-collection or habitat destruction. One reason why orchids are more vulnerable than other plants is that the process of seed germination is very easily disturbed.

The slow process of germination
Each orchid fruit can produce several million tiny seeds. But, unlike most plants, these seeds have no food store on which the seedling can feed during germination. The orchids are completely dependent on fungi, especially during germination (but also throughout their lives), to obtain nutrients for them.

The fungus lives protected in the seed, and later in the roots of the plant. The fungus absorbs nourishment from decaying leaves and other dead vegetation, and passes it on to the orchid. This type of partnership, in which both sides benefit, is called *symbiosis*. Despite the help from the fungi, it usually takes several years before a seed grows sufficiently mature to produce a flowering stem. So if, during this process, the soil around is disturbed, for example by ploughing, this is likely to interfere with this long maturing process.

You will find there is a great ▶ **variety of curious flower designs in the orchid family. The basic features are shown in these illustrations of the common spotted orchid.**

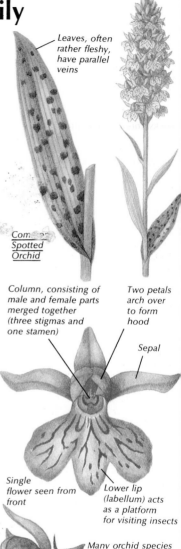

Leaves, often rather fleshy, have parallel veins

Common Spotted Orchid

Column, consisting of male and female parts merged together (three stigmas and one stamen)

Two petals arch over to form hood

Sepal

Single flower seen from front

Lower lip (labellum) acts as a platform for visiting insects

Single flower seen from side

Many orchid species have a spur filled with nectar. This singles out insect-pollinators with long probosces ("tong

The pollen

Since orchids have very efficient and advanced methods of being pollinated, they have only one stamen. In the more primitive orchids such as the helleborines, the pollen is produced in a mass, held together by sticky threads. The more advanced species – in fact most of the other orchids – produce pollen in a few lumps called *pollinia*. The pollinia have sticky stalks which attach themselves to the pollinator's head or tongue when it visits the flower.

Orchids which mimic insects

There is a strange sub-group or genus in the orchid family, known as *Ophrys*, found mainly in southern Europe. These flowers provide no nectar to entice pollinating insects. Instead the lower lipped petal looks, feels and smells exactly like the female of certain insects. Different species of orchids of course mimic different species of insects.

When a male insect of the same species visits these flowers, he is so struck by the similarity of the lower petal to his partner that he tries to mate with it. As he does so, he picks up the pollinia on his head. When he visits another flower the pollinia are transferred to the stigmas, carrying out pollination.

So with these flowers, the visiting insects are not after food but are trying to satisfy their sexual needs.

The fly orchid mimics the female ▶ of certain wasp species. A visiting wasp is fooled into trying to mate with the lower lipped petal and, in doing so, pollinia stick to its head. The bee orchids (illustrated on page 45) are also members of the *Ophrys* genus, and mimic certain bee species.

Proboscis seeks nectar in spur. Pollinia stick to proboscis.

Burnet moth visiting flower

▲ The pyramidal orchid is pollinated by butterflies and moths, whose long probosces (or "tongues") can reach into the spur to obtain the nectar. As they do this, the pollinia stick to the proboscis and are carried to another flower.

Lower lip looks like female wasp

Male wasp tries to mate with lower lip

Pollinia

Wasp flies away with pollinia stuck to its head

FLOWER HABITATS
Why plants grow where they do

On the following pages (44–57) you will find descriptions of the main European habitats, where you will find strikingly different plant communities. These pages should help you to find out *what* plants are characteristic of these habitats, and, more importantly, *why* they grow there – especially when there are so many other habitats with more favourable conditions for plant growth.

The link between families of plants and habitats
In some habitats, several species from the same family may be found. This is often because members of that family share a special feature which equips them, above all others, to cope with the conditions there.

For example the pea family has a special characteristic which enables its members to survive in poor soil such as on heathlands (see pages 35–36 and 46–47).

The effect of the environment on plant shapes
Most habitats are shared by a large range of species, from many different families. But very often, even though they are unrelated and have very different *flowers*, their pattern of growth makes them look similar. This is because conditions in the habitat make a certain shape and pattern of growth necessary for survival there. For example, plants of high mountains tend to be low-growing – all seeming to hide from the extremes of wind and cold (see pages 56–57).

Do plants choose their particular habitat?
It is hardly ever true to say that plants grow in a particular spot because they "like" it there. What plant would choose to live at the top of a windswept mountain if it could find a spot in some fertile lowland region? Why stand in the sticky mud of an estuary and get drowned twice a day by the tides?

The answer is that by living in these grim habitats, they avoid competition from other more aggressive plants that cannot cope with such extreme conditions but that are keen fighters for space in more favourable places.

Plants compete for survival in a similar way to animals. It is easy to understand how animals competing for food will also have to compete for areas in which to hunt and graze. The strongest species will get the food first and the weaker species will have to find something else to eat, go elsewhere, or die.

In the plant world, for example, as a tree grows larger it casts shade on the plants growing below. If certain species cannot survive in the shade they must move out into the meadow and fight for a patch of soil with all the other species. If the competition is too great, they must go elsewhere or die.

If an animal or plant species can cope with a tough environment it will find a refuge away from the battleground of competition. The tough environment it finds may be in acid bogs (illustrated opposite), in the mountains, out along the coast, or deep in a shady wood.

Despite the competition, many more favourable habitats such as meadows have a wonderful variety of species, all surviving together in harmony. This is because each of them requires something different from the environment, or because their life cycles are staggered so each species flowers and fruits at a different time. In this way they do not have to compete. The struggle for survival means that every plant which survives, wherever it may be, has done so by finding a "niche".

How habitats may change

When you explore any habitat, do not imagine that it will always remain the same. Apart from the seasons, all sorts of changes take place. Bare patches of ground become carpeted with weeds, old trees eventually die allowing light to flood into a shady wood, land may suffer drought or flood, or be buried beneath an avalanche. These are all natural changes, quite apart from those brought about by people interfering with the habitat.

Some of these changes are sudden and dramatic, but most of them take place gradually. Plant communities can adjust to cope with many of these changes – some species will die out while others take the opportunity to move in.

Plant succession

If most habitats are left undisturbed, the vegetation will develop in a particular pattern. For example, if grassland is left unmown or ungrazed, it will be invaded first by scrub and eventually by woodland. Similarly, if wetland is left undisturbed, reeds will gradually help dry up the water, scrub will follow, and finally wet woodland will become established.

This natural replacement of some plants by others is called *succession*. The type of vegetation which is the last to develop, and which can last for hundreds of years, is called *climax vegetation*. The natural climax vegetation over most of Europe is forest, the type depending on local climate and soils.

▼ **Plants have less competition from other species if they can adapt to an unfavourable habitat such as the bog with its soggy acid soil shown below.**

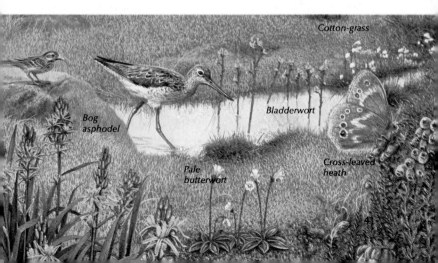

Cotton-grass

Bog asphodel

Bladderwort

Pale butterwort

Cross-leaved heath

41

Wasteland weeds

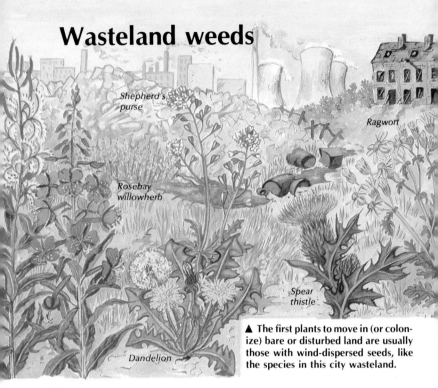

Shepherd's purse

Ragwort

Rosebay willowherb

Spear thistle

Dandelion

▲ The first plants to move in (or colonize) bare or disturbed land are usually those with wind-dispersed seeds, like the species in this city wasteland.

The land has been disturbed by people for centuries, but never more so than in the twentieth century. Areas of bare land are created all the time – on ploughed fields, embankments along highways, heavily trampled paths, gravel drives, flower beds, demolition sites and waste tips. All these places, and many others, can be called "wasteland". They all provide fresh areas for plants to colonize. Plants that move in first are known as "weeds".

Wasteland may not seem a very exciting habitat to start this section, but they are easily explored since most people pass by them every day. Wasteland can demonstrate a lot about the struggle for life amongst plants and the dispersal of seeds.

Characteristics of weeds

If you list the species found on newly-disturbed land you will find that most of them have wind-dispersed seeds. Other types of seeds may already have been present in the soil, and some may have been lying dormant for several years. But many of the plants will be those whose seeds can fly for miles on the wind – willowherbs and members of the daisy family (Compositae) such as thistles and ragworts.

The weeds seen growing most abundantly will be species which produce lots of seedlings. Often these plants produce so many flowers and seeds that they have no energy left for storing food over the winter. So many early colonizers die once they have set seed – for example the annual poppies, the biennial spear thistle and the ephemeral shepherd's purse. *Annuals* take one year to complete their life cycle, *biennials* take two years, and *ephemerals* have such a fast life cycle that they can fit in several within a season.

Survival of the early colonizers

These short-lived plants *depend* on setting seed for their survival, so most ensure that self-fertilization is possible if cross-pollination fails (see pages 15–18). Their seeds must also be sure to find bare soil on which to germinate, and there is plenty of bare soil on wasteland in its first few years.

But as more plants invade and spread on wasteland, the bare soil is taken up. Then only *perennial* plants which can store food over the winter and live for several years, will survive.

Succession of plants

So wasteland vegetation gradually changes. At first dominated by wind-dispersed annuals which produce lots of seeds, it later becomes dominated by perennials, notably grasses, which save their energy for over-wintering instead of spending it all on producing flowers and seeds. For example, the annual poppy will be squeezed out, but creeping thistles, being perennial and able to compete for space, will survive the change. This natural change is called plant succession (see page 41).

The history of weeds

Wasteland became a commonly seen habitat comparatively recently, since it occurs as a result of human activities. Yet weeds have been around a lot longer than humans. This is because wasteland sites do occur as a result of natural activity such as landslides, melting glaciers and erupting volcanoes. But bare areas produced in this way are quite rare, so many of the weeds that are now common were rare species before humans populated the earth.

▼ Cornfields, when ploughed up for sowing, provide wasteland conditions. Annuals like these poppies, charlock and mayweed may move in, giving splashes of colour amongst the wheat crop. Unfortunately, they are rarely seen, now that purer grain is sown and herbicides are used to kill "unwanted" weeds.

43

Chalk and limestone

The open grassland of chalk and limestone has perhaps the richest variety of flowering plants found in any habitat.

The soils
The soils that develop on chalk and limestone are known as *calcareous* soils. They are shallow and not necessarily very nutritious for plants, but they tend to be warm, being quite dry, and rich in calcium carbonate which gives them a sweet or, more correctly, *alkaline* flavour.

Most plants prefer the more alkaline soils to sour *acid* soils (see "Moors and heaths" overleaf). There are some species which can grow *only* on very calcareous soils: these are called "calcicoles".

So a rich variety of plants may grow on chalk and limestone, even in one small area. This is because no one species can become abundant enough to dominate, due to the rather unnutritious soil.

Typical plants
It is difficult to generalize about the characteristic plants, since chalk and limestone grasslands have such a wide range: they occur both in mountains and at sea level along the coast, in northern Scandinavia and on the shores of the Mediterranean. But you will always find enough "calcicoles" to indicate the soil type. Look for rockrose, salad burnet, dropwort, hoary plantain, certain orchids such as pyramidal, fragrant and bee, and grasses such as yellow oat and quaking. All these and the plants illustrated below indicate chalk and limestone areas, since they cannot grow on any other type of soil.

Grazing by animals
The rich variety of plants remains as long as the grasslands are grazed by animals. This keeps down the taller coarser plants and allows plenty of light to reach the turf. If there are

▼ The calcicoles shown below can grow on quite heavily grazed grassland. Some, like the fairy flax and squinancywort, are often too tiny to spot. But if you lie down (beware of the prickly stemless thistle!), armed with a hand lens, you will see them.

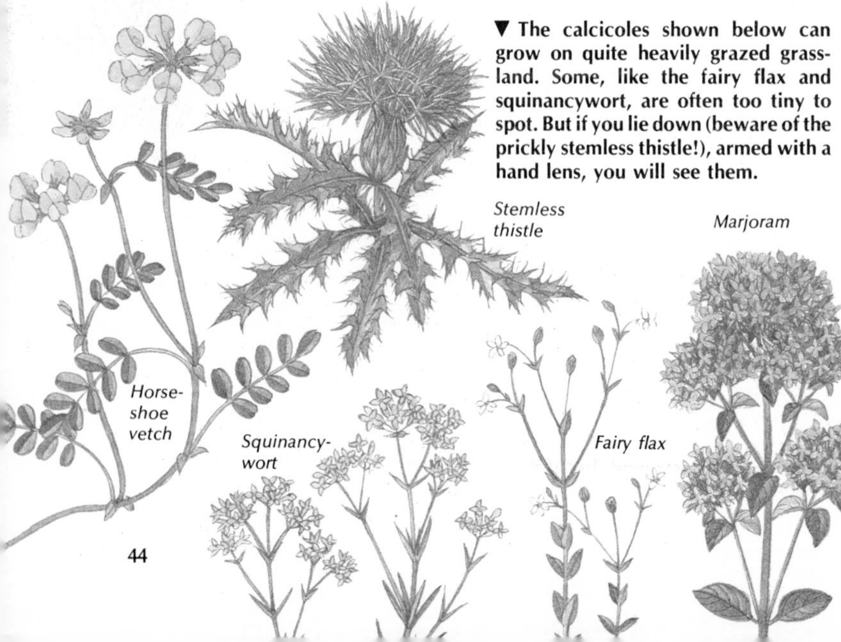

Horse-shoe vetch

Squinancy-wort

Stemless thistle

Fairy flax

Marjoram

Bee orchids
look like the
Eucera bees
which they
attract to carry
out pollination

Quaking
grass ▶

Birdsfoot trefoil

▲ Bee orchids and quaking grass are "calcicoles" which flourish in lightly grazed grassland. Many orchids, including pyramidal and fragrant, are also "calcicoles".

few grazing animals on the grass-land, taller grasses such as false brome tend to overwhelm the smaller plants. Grazing will of course destroy some of the flowers, but most of the plants are perennial (see page 25) and can survive for several years without setting seed. The right balance of grazing is important: if grassland is too heavily grazed some plants may be destroyed, but if it is too light, coarse plants take over.

Trees and shrubs

If the grassland is not grazed at all, scrub soon invades and blocks out light so many species are forced out. Some bushes and trees characteristic of chalk and limestone are box and yew (both evergreen), wayfaring tree, whitebeam, dogwood, and also traveller's joy whose fluffy fruits (old man's beard) are seen in autumn.

Moors and heaths

Bell heather

Heather (or ling)

Cross-leaved heath

Wavy hair-grass

Cotton-grass

▲ Heathers dominate on all but the wettest moors and heaths, where grasses and sedges tend to take over. Heather (ling) is the most dominant species, found with bell heather on very dry heathland, and sometimes with cross-leaved heath on moors and wet heaths.

Europe's vast open expanses of heathland and moorland have a very special wildness. Most of them were once forests which were felled centuries ago, and where trees have been prevented from returning. On many heaths and moors grazing by animals has stopped the natural regeneration of trees. But some moors and heaths are ancient, naturally-formed landscapes: this is especially true of those on mountains above the treeline, and in windswept coastal districts where trees cannot grow.

The rolling expanses of heather, turning purple and mauve when it flowers in late summer, give the moors and heaths their character.

The difference between moors and heaths

You may have wondered what distinguishes a moor from a heath, since both have similar vegetation. The broad definition is that moorlands occur in upland areas on damp, acid, peaty soils, while heathlands occur in lowland areas on dry, acid, sandy soils. So their similarity is due to their *acid substrate*. Substrate is a useful word which can mean solid rock, pure sand and raw compost as well as other soils. *Bogs* also have an acid substrate and boggy areas are found on both heaths and moors.

The acid soil

Whether dry and sandy or damp and peaty, this acid soil has few nutrients and is distasteful to all but a few plants. Species belonging to the heather family (Ericaceae), and some grasses and sedges, thrive on acid soil, so they tend to dominate on moors and heaths.

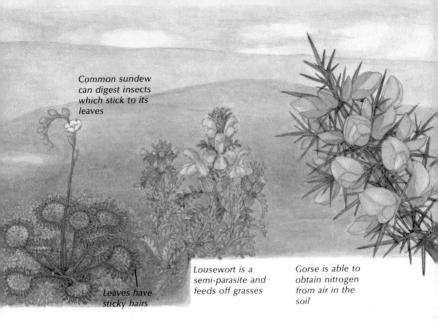

Common sundew can digest insects which stick to its leaves

Leaves have sticky hairs

Lousewort is a semi-parasite and feeds off grasses

Gorse is able to obtain nitrogen from air in the soil

The heathers that dominate

When the heather species bloom in late summer, heathland and moorland become a haze of pinks and purples. The flowers supply great quantities of nectar for insects, especially bees for whom heather is a favourite flower. Since there are few other plants in flower around, heather has the full attention of insects and a very good success rate for pollination.

Heaths and moors tend to have fairly cool and moist conditions, since they are found mainly near the sea and heather thrives in these. But it is also well-adapted to cope with any variations and extremes. Its leaves are both tiny and rolled up, which helps prevent water loss during dry periods and frost damage in winter. Also, being evergreen, it does not need to spend valuable time developing leaves each spring, and can therefore survive in cloudy upland regions where the growing season is short.

▲ The acid soils of moors and heaths are poor in nutrients, so many plants growing here get the nutrients they need from sources other than the soil.

Other plants

Moorland and heathland substrates are very poor in plant nutrients. Species belonging to the pea family (Leguminosae), such as gorse, birds-foot trefoil and vetches, can grow here since they can obtain nitrogen from air in the soil (see pages 35–36).

The semi-parasitic plants such as louseworts are found, especially on the moors (see figworts page 37). These plants can get nourishment from grasses, mainly fescue and the attractive wavy hair-grass.

On wetter ground, especially in bogs, insectivorous plants like the sundews and butterworts grow: the poor soil does not matter to them since they can supplement their diet by digesting tiny insects which get stuck to their leaves.

Coasts

The seaside is always fun to visit, but coastal habitats provide quite difficult conditions for plant life. Those that can grow here are fascinating, having special features in order to survive the drought, salt, and often lack of nutrients.

Types of coastline

Europe's coastline varies enormously, from high cliffs to flat coastal marshlands riddled with estuaries and creeks. The shore itself may consist of platforms of rocks or boulders, shingle, rolling sand dunes or acres of oozing mud.

All these habitats have one thing in common – they are all exposed to high winds and strong sunshine.

Drought conditions

Coastal sites do not usually have such extremes of temperature as areas inland. The strong sun and wind however dry everything out. This, together with the fact that most coastal substrates – sand, shingle, rock – cannot retain water, means that drought is a common condition on the coast. Thirst-making salt all around adds to the problems. So one of the most important features of coastal vegetation is being able to conserve water.

It is not that coastal plants *prefer* the severe conditions of drought and salt, but the few that can cope have an advantage: they have escaped from the competition between species in more favourable habitats inland, where the majority of other plants dominate.

Saltmarshes

Mud, the finest substrate of all, collects only along coasts which are quite sheltered from pounding waves. Large areas of mudflats and sand flats are often found in the mouths of estuaries and behind spits and bars (thin strips of land jutting into the sea parallel with the shore). The plant community which grows on mud and sand flats is known as saltmarsh.

At first it seems odd that a saltmarsh should have a drought problem, since it is drenched twice a day by the highest tides. But salty water is very thirst-making. What is worse, saltmarsh mud is even saltier than the sea itself, especially on sunny, windy days when pure water will evaporate from the marsh, leaving salt crystals behind. Few plants therefore can grow here and those that do have features rather similar to those found on the dry sand dunes (see pages 50–51).

One remarkable thing about saltmarsh flowers is that they are not damaged by their regular drowning

▼ Thrift is an adaptable coastal plant, growing, often in profusion, on saltmarsh, shingle, rock and on cliffs. It is also found on mountains.

Dense rosette of succulent leaves helps it to retain water

in salt water. But their *pollen* may be destroyed at high tide, so the anthers must close tightly whenever the flower is submerged.

At low tide when the marsh dries out, the flowers are visited by hoards of bees and butterflies. Notice how the flowering times of each species are spread out over the summer with little overlap. This ensures that each species has a good chance of being pollinated, by having, for most of its flowering period, the full attention of the insects. In June, thrift flowers carpet the marsh with pink. Pink turns to mauve in July and August when the sea lavender takes over. By the end of August the flowers of sea aster take their turn, continuing through into September.

Leaves are scale-like and succulent to store water

Can take root within three days if mud is not too wet

▲ Glasswort is one of the first plants to colonize the mud, helping to stabilize the shifting mud so that other salt-marsh plants can move in.

▼ A typical saltmarsh. Cord-grass is another early colonizer of the mud. Sea aster often grows in carpets over the saltmarsh, since there is little competition from other species. Sea purslane, like most saltmarsh plants, is a perennial so it will not lose its footing in the mud by dying after setting seed.

Sea aster

Cord-grass

Sea purslane

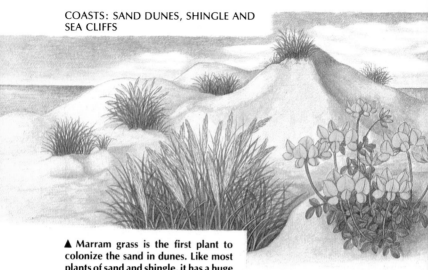

▲ Marram grass is the first plant to colonize the sand in dunes. Like most plants of sand and shingle, it has a huge root system to seek out every drop of moisture. If covered by sand, it can still grow up through it: this feature helps it to stabilize shifting sand so other plants can move in. It copes with very dry weather by rolling up its leaves to prevent too much water loss.

▲ Birdsfoot trefoil can survive in the dry acid soils of sand and shingle, which are often poor in nitrates, a nutrient which plants need. Being a member of the pea family (see pages 35–36), it can obtain nitrates in other ways.

Sand dunes and shingle beaches

More of Europe's coastline consists of sand and shingle shores than any other type. The most interesting stretches are those where the sand or shingle has built up into a series of ridges parallel with the sea – either dunes of wind-blown sand, or storm-crests of wave-tossed shingle. Here coastal plants may be found quite far inland, until they meet competition from other species.

Both sand and shingle are unable to retain water – it washes straight through, carrying any nutrients with it. The tops of the dunes and crests are therefore extremely dry, acid and poor in nutrients, but nevertheless you may find a few plants here.

But look in the dips or troughs between the ridges for the richest variety of plants. The troughs often collect water, nutrients, and shell fragments rich in lime, making them more alkaline. In dunes these troughs are called *slacks*.

If you walk over the dunes inland from the sea, you will follow the stages by which vegetation has developed, a process called succession (see page 41). The bare sand nearest the sea becomes colonized by marram grass. The farther you walk from the sea, the older the dunes are; so vegetation will have had longer to develop on the older dunes, and will be more varied. As the vegetation dies back each

▲ Viper's bugloss grows in dune slacks where shell fragments have accumulated, making the sand more alkaline, and where there are more nutrients.

Sea cliffs
Few flowering plants can grow out of solid rock, but on the tops and lower ledges of cliffs, out of reach of pounding waves, a glorious variety of species may be found.

Here shallow soil forms, and conditions are easier for plants than they are on shingle, sandy and muddy shores. But the sea winds are strong and full of salt, and only some inland species can grow here. So you will find on cliffs a fascinating mixture of coastal and inland plants as well as those characteristic of mountain tops, such as thrift (see page 48). The richest variety of all grows on chalk and limestone cliffs (see pages 44–45).

▼ Sea campion, like many coastal plants, grows low on the ground to shelter from the drying wind: only the flowers are held on longish stalks to attract insect-pollinators. Its waxy leaves help prevent water loss.

English stonecrop can cling to the barest of rocky ledges. Being a succulent plant, it can store water in its leaves which helps it to survive the sun, wind and salt spray.

winter, it adds organic material to the sand. This organic matter improves conditions for plants by helping to retain water and adding nutrients to the sand.

Eventually conditions on the older dunes become so much better for plants that species that are less well-adapted to the coast can move in, and so can scrub. These gradually push the coastal plants out.

If you walk back inland from the sea over shingle ridges, the same build-up of vegetation can be observed: the older the shingle ridge, the thicker and more varied the vegetation you will find growing on it.

Sea campion

English stonecrop

51

Wetlands and freshwater

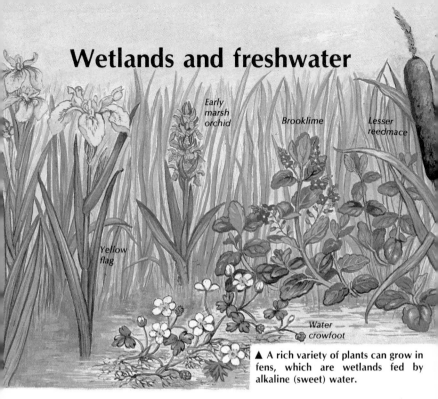

Early marsh orchid

Brooklime

Lesser reedmace

Yellow flag

Water crowfoot

▲ A rich variety of plants can grow in fens, which are wetlands fed by alkaline (sweet) water.

Watery places can harbour a wealth of colourful flowers, especially in summer. Look for these along riverbanks, around lakes and ponds, in marshes, bogs and damp meadows. You will find different types of plants according to the amount of water, and to its type – acid or alkaline.

Wetlands: marshes, bogs, fens

You may have wondered what the difference is between these types of wetland. The different types of wetland are determined by their soil and water.

Marsh is a more general term for wetland, but, unlike bogs and fens, marsh soils have very little organic material, and no peat at all. Peat is dead plant material which is only partially decayed.

Bogs are *acid* and, just as on moors and heaths (see pages 46–47), the acid conditions limit the variety of plants which can grow. On bogs, look out for cotton-grass, mosses, members of the heather family such as cross-leaved heath and cranberry and the strange insectivorous plants like the sundews and butterworts.

Fens are fed with *alkaline* water draining from chalk and limestone hills. So, like chalk and limestone grassland (see pages 44–45), a rich variety of plants can grow on fens.

All types of wetlands are threatened habitats, especially fenland which, once drained, provides valuable agricultural land.

Wetland plants as "indicators"

When you visit any habitat, notice

how dramatically the vegetation changes wherever there is a lot of water. Wetland plants can indicate extra moisture in the soil when you are out walking. Often the strong smell of water mint leaves, crushed underfoot, is the first warning of soggy ground on an apparently dry path. A ribbon of yellow marsh marigolds may pick out the course of a tiny stream cutting through a field.

Plants of open water

Most aquatic plants hold their flowers above water for pollination, usually by insects. Notice how many water plants have submerged leaves which look different from those above water. In fact the underwater leaves often look more like green roots. This is because they are very finely divided in order to flow freely with the moving water, and yet still have a good surface area for carrying out photosynthesis.

Wetland succession

The pond illustrated below will not naturally remain the same size or depth over the years. Open water will give way to reeds which in turn give way to scrub, in the following stages.

1. Every autumn dead vegetation builds up at the bottom of the pond. There is so little air here that the vegetation does not decompose properly, and forms layers of peat.

2. The water gradually becomes shallower and the fringe of *reeds* spreads in towards the centre of the pond. This forces plants of open water into yet deeper water to avoid being overshadowed by reeds.

3. Wetland scrub, called *carr*, consisting of alders, willows and buckthorns, moves into the reed bed, shading out the reeds.

This is another example of plant succession, which eventually leads to the pond drying out and the wetland scrub taking over.

3. Carr (wetland scrub)

2. Reed bed

1. Open water

Woodlands

When you visit an area, the type of trees growing there can tell you a lot about local conditions. For instance, most willows grow only on damp soils, while birch prefers well-drained, usually sandy soils. Ash and beech favour nutrient-rich alkaline ground, while many pines grow better in acid soil with few nutrients.

Conifers are usually hardier than broadleaved trees, and better able to withstand cold and drought. Conifers are therefore found further north and at higher altitudes, and also on very dry coastal districts.

Looking for flowers in woods

Deciduous woods are the most rewarding for plant hunters. Few plants grow in evergreen woods, especially coniferous ones which produce a deep acid litter of needles in which hardly any plants can grow, even if light could penetrate the wood.

But keep a look-out for flowers such as bugle and trailing St John's wort in the open glades and edges of walks and rides in all woods. Natural woods, as opposed to plantations, include trees of different ages and have open spaces where old trees have died and fallen. So natural woods contain the greatest variety of flowers.

▲ Primroses, being perennials, use the food stored in their roots to produce leaves early in the year (see page 25). They are therefore able to flower in spring before the woodland floor becomes shaded by the leaf canopy above.

Deciduous woods in spring

Primroses, violets and bluebells are the most well-known woodland flowers. They all flower in spring. This is not just a coincidence: most woodland plants time their life cycle so they flower before the canopy of leaves above shades the woodland floor. So, by avoiding competition from the hundreds of plants which need summer sunshine and must fight for space in the open, woodland flowers find a refuge.

In fact they have so little competition from other species that they grow in huge numbers. Primroses, bluebells and wood anemones often grow in carpets on the more acid soils; ramsons and lily-of-the-valley often carpet the more alkaline woodland soils.

▼ This tiny spring-flowering plant, moschatel, is often overlooked in woods. It is also called "town hall clock" because it has four clock-like faces.

Uses adhesive roots to climb trees

Adult leaf has smooth edge

Juvenile leaf is lobed

It is difficult for ivy to photosynthes- ▶ ize in summer when the tree canopy casts shade. But, being evergreen, it builds up food when the trees have lost their leaves and light enters the wood. In winter ivy's foliage provides shelter for birds in the otherwise bare wood, and the berries supply food.

Plants that can live in shade

During summer, although the full leaf canopy casts shade, a small amount of light can filter through, so you will usually find some plants growing below. Some species have features which enable them to live in shady places.

Ivy and honeysuckle are climbers and can reach light by climbing trees. Their flowers are borne only on stems which have found their way into some light.

Look at the leaves of plants which can grow in shade as well as sun – bramble, ground ivy or stinging nettle: you may find the leaves in the shade are larger than those in the sun, so as to catch more light.

A few species use another source of energy instead of light to produce food, in the same way that fungi do. These are either saprophytic (feeding on decaying matter), or parasitic (feeding on living plants or animals). Yellow bird's-nest, for example, is a saprophyte found in beech and pine woods.

Tree flowers

All trees except conifers bear flowers. Catkins are usually produced in late winter or early spring, before the foliage develops. The leaves would prevent pollen from moving freely in the wind (see pages 13–14). Blossoms usually flower later in the year, when the highest numbers of pollinating insects are about.

▼ Notice how similar these two woodland flowers look, though wild strawberry is a herb and hawthorn is a tree. Both species belong to the Rose family (see page 32).

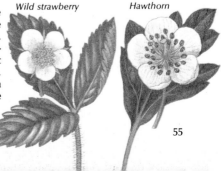

Wild strawberry   Hawthorn

Mountains

Look for these different zones as you climb a mountain, but bear in mind that most of the trees may have been cleared. ▶

Peaks sometimes frozen all year. Above a certain level, no plants grow.

Turf thins out. Crag and scree with flowers.

Alpine meadows – no trees

Treeline

Coniferous forest (pasture if trees cleared)

Mixed forest

The mountains, with their fresh air and glorious scenery, are very enjoyable places in which to look for flowers.

As in most habitats, the variety of plants will depend on the soil, which in turn depends on the rock below and on the climate. See "Chalk and limestone" and "Heaths and moors" (pages 44–47) for information about the difference between alkaline and acid soils and rocks. In the limestone mountains of southern Europe, with its sunnier climate, the plants are richer in variety than in the cool, wet granite hills of northern Scotland.

The lower pastures and forests
As you wend your way uphill you may pass through many different habitats. The illustration shows broadly the types of vegetation which occur naturally at different altitudes. Both coniferous and broadleaved woodland may be found lower down, but further up only conifers can survive. But in both these zones the trees may have been cleared, leaving pastures.

If the lower slopes are not wooded, try to decide why not. Is it because the forest has been cleared? Is the vegetation being grazed too heavily, preventing trees and shrubs from growing up? Has there been an avalanche in the last century? Or is the climate so wet and cool that acid blanket bog (see "Wetlands" pages 52–53) has developed, as it has in large areas of Scotland. Very few plants can grow on these acid blanket bogs.

The level at which the conifer trees thin out and stop growing is called the treeline. It is interesting to compare the different bands of vegetation on opposite sides of a valley. On south-facing slopes, which are generally warmer and sunnier for longer periods of the year, the treeline is usually higher up than on the north-facing slopes, where the snow lies for longer.

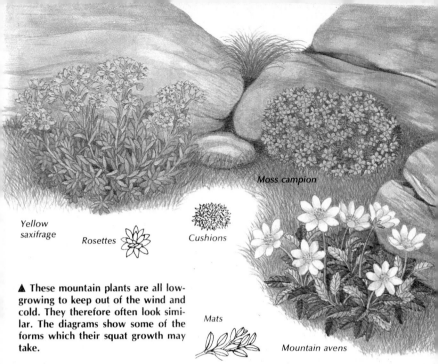

Yellow saxifrage

Rosettes

Cushions

Moss campion

Mats

Mountain avens

▲ These mountain plants are all low-growing to keep out of the wind and cold. They therefore often look similar. The diagrams show some of the forms which their squat growth may take.

Higher up the mountains – the alpine meadows

As you walk out above the lush meadows and forest and above the treeline, the turf gets shorter. The flowers are often large compared with the rest of the plant. Look out for flowers belonging to the gentian, primrose and buttercup families. These are often seen bursting into flower before the snow around them has completely melted. The flowers must get off to an early start with such a short growing season ahead of them before the snow returns.

The mountain peaks

The turf begins to thin out further up. More low-growing plants festoon the crags and scree, but sometimes you will need to hunt among the boulders to see them. These plants must grow low so as to keep out the wind and avoid damage by

frost and wind; another reason for this is that they have only a short summer season in which to grow.

Though their squat growth makes all the plants look rather similar, there is a great variety of species from several different families, and their flowers vary enormously in glorious colours and designs. This is because many mountain plants are insect-pollinated. But at very high altitudes, especially in the mountains of northern Europe, weather conditions may sometimes be too severe for insects to survive. So the further north you are, the more you find that mountain plants are pollinated by wind rather than by insects. Those that are insect-pollinated have devices to ensure that self-pollination takes place in case cross-pollination fails (see page 18). Most of them rely heavily on vegetative reproduction (see page 26).

The field botanist

You can learn something about the natural world from books, but it is much more exciting and informative to build on this knowledge by exploring for yourself.

All habitats and their wild plants and animals are threatened with extinction because of human activities. In order to try and conserve them, we should understand as much about them as possible. This book is only an introduction to the flowering plants, but it may have suggested ways of looking at them in the wild, and of understanding how and why they grow where they do.

Understanding more about plants

Wherever you go, try not to take the plants around you for granted. Ask yourself questions: what species are these? How did they get here? Why these species and not others? How do they survive and how long will they stay? What creatures live amongst them? The answers will not always be obvious, but you will begin to learn to interpret what you see.

How to use a hand lens: Hold the lens steady and close to your eye. Bring the flower into focus by moving closer.

Looking at flowers

Never pick flowers – many species have become extinct through over-picking. When identifying, take the book to the flower not the flower to the book (see page 62 for suggested field guides). Try to carry a hand lens to observe tiny features. *Naming* the species should not be an end in itself – use it as a key to discover more information. Most books indicate a plant's usual habitats. After a while you will be able to use flowering plants as indicators of local conditions. You can also use the hand lens to find out how a flower is pollinated. Is the flower dichogamous (see page 16)? What kind of pollinator is it designed to attract? You may well be able to observe the pollinating insects at work.

▼ Two sketches of the same heathland area both made in August: the one on the left was made two years after a fire, the one on the right three years after that. Notice the changes. You can record them in the way suggested opposite.

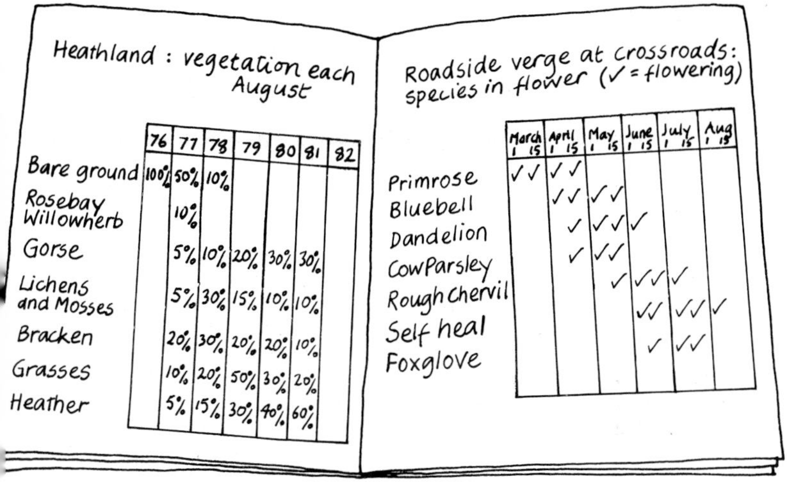

Heathland : vegetation each August

	76	77	78	79	80	81	82
Bare ground	100%	50%	10%				
Rosebay Willowherb		10%					
Gorse			5%	10%	20%	30%	30%
Lichens and Mosses			5%	30%	15%	10%	10%
Bracken			20%	30%	20%	20%	10%
Grasses			10%	20%	50%	30%	20%
Heather			5%	15%	30%	40%	60%

Roadside verge at crossroads: species in flower (✓ = flowering)

	March 1	March 15	April 1	April 15	May 1	May 15	June 1	June 15	July 1	July 15	Aug 1	Aug 15
Primrose	✓	✓	✓	✓								
Bluebell			✓	✓	✓	✓	✓					
Dandelion					✓	✓	✓					
Cow Parsley						✓	✓	✓				
Rough Chervil								✓	✓	✓	✓	
Self heal										✓	✓	✓
Foxglove										✓	✓	✓

▲ **Recording yearly changes:** In the dry summer of 1976 fire destroyed vast areas of this piece of heathland. Nothing survived immediately after the fire, but over the following years heathland vegetation slowly grew back. The record above shows in what order and in what quantities each species returned. Each August the same area was visited and the *percentage* of ground covered by each species was estimated and recorded. Each new species as it occurred was added to the bottom of the list.

▲ **Recording short-term changes:** A similar method can be used to record weekly or monthly events. Try looking at the flowering sequence along a roadside verge. This record shows both how long each species was in flower and the variety in flower at the same time.

Notice how the flowering periods of closely-related species, such as those in the cow parsley family, hardly ever overlap. This makes sure that each species has good chance of being pollinated.

Recording changes in habitats

If you are able to make several visits to a habitat, however small, you can learn a lot by recording changes which take place – two methods are illustrated above. If your area is interfered with by humans in any way, make a note of what happened (for example heathland burned, a hedge cut, a pasture ploughed) and carry on recording how the plants respond.

Looking at flowers on holiday

Before you go on holiday, try and find out what sort of plants you might expect to find in the place you will be visiting. What is the local geology like? Is the area renowned for any special or rare plants? If the habitats in your holiday area are unfamiliar, think what their important features might be and how the plants might be adapted to cope with conditions.

59

FURTHER INFORMATION
Famous botanical sites

Wherever you are in Britain, you will be able to find at least a few wild flowers, and there are hundreds of places where a wide selection can be seen. Some sites, because of their position and geology, have an exceptional variety and a few of these are listed below.

Most of them are nature reserves and permits may be required to visit them. Visitors should stay on rights of way and not pick, uproot or otherwise disturb the plants; make sure your visit does not spoil the site for other people.

Further details of interesting sites in Britain are given in books such as "Finding Wild Flowers" by R. S. R. Fitter, published by Collins, and in the Nature Guides, published by Usborne.

CHALK AND LIMESTONE
CHALK:
North and **South Downs** of south-east England, particularly Kent and Sussex.
LIMESTONE:
Cotswolds, Gloucestershire.
Derbyshire Dales.
Wye Valley, Gloucestershire and Herefordshire.
Avon Gorge, Avon.
Upper Teesdale, Durham.
Mendip Hills in Somerset, for example **Cheddar Gorge** and **Brean Down**.
Ormes Head, Gwynedd, north Wales.
Gower Peninsula, West Glamorgan, south Wales.
Durness, Highland Region, Scotland.
Limestone "pavements" (bare fissured rock) are found in **Cumbria**, the **Craven** district of the Pennines in Yorkshire, and in **The Burren**, Co. Clare, Ireland.

LOWLAND HEATHLAND
The **Breckland** of Norfolk and Suffolk (around Thetford) – heathland and chalk grassland are mixed here.
New Forest, Hampshire.
Dorset heaths, for example Studland and Wareham.
Lizard Peninsula, Cornwall (on serpentine rock).
Coastal heaths of **Suffolk**.

COASTAL SITES
Lizard Peninsula, Cornwall (also listed under "Lowland heathland".
Ormes Head, Gwynedd, north Wales, and the **Gower Peninsula**, West Glamorgan, south Wales, both also listed under "Limestone".
Isles of Scilly
SAND DUNES:
Braunton Burrows, Devon.
Isle of Anglesey, Gwynedd, north Wales.
Southport to **Formby**, Lancashire.
The **Lincolnshire** coast.
North Norfolk coast (dunes, shingle and saltmarsh occurs from **Hunstanton** to **Sheringham**).
Machair on the sandy west coasts of the **Western Isles**, Scotland.
SALTMARSHES:
Essex, south **Suffolk**, the **Thames Estuary** (Kent and Essex), and the **Wash** (Lincolnshire/Norfolk).
SHINGLE:
North Norfolk (see under "Sand dunes" above).
Chesil beach, Dorset.
Dungeness, Kent.

WETLANDS:
Canals, meres and bogs of **Shrop-** and **Cheshire.**
The **Norfolk Broads**, for example **Ranworth Broad**. Fens and marshes of East Anglia, for example **Wicken Fen**, Cambridgeshire.
Sedgemoor, Somerset.

WOODLANDS
Highlands of **Kerry** and **Cork**, Ireland, where Lusitanian species occur (ie. species found chiefly in Spain and Portugal).
Derbyshire ashwoods.
Oak and mixed woods of the **Weald**, especially in Kent and Sussex.
Epping Forest, Essex.
Forest of Dean, Gloucestershire.

MOUNTAINS
Ben Lawers, Highland Region, Scotland: this is the most important site in Britain for arctic-alpine plants.
Cairngorms, Highland and Grampian Regions, Scotland.
Snowdonia, north Wales.
Lake District, Cumbria.
Donegal, Ireland, where arctic-alpine plants occur near sea level.

▼ **Though Britain has a relatively limited number of plant species, some of the sites listed above are of international interest. Every country of course has its specialities, and very rich sites can be found in other parts of Europe. Shown below is an alpine meadow in the Pyrenees, Andorra.**

Useful addresses

One of the best ways of learning more about the countryside is to go out with others. Some societies arrange field days; the leader may be a specialist or an all-round naturalist.

Wild Flower Society, 68 Outwoods Road, Loughborough, Leicestershire LE11 3LY. Members keep a diary to record where and when species are seen in flower. These diaries can be submitted in a competition to find out who saw most species in flower each year.

Botanical Society of the British Isles, c/o Dept. of Botany, British Museum (Natural History), Cromwell Road, London SW7 5BD. A more learned society which encourages junior members and amateurs and anyone involved in research (such as the records suggested on pages 58–59).

County Naturalists' Trust. You can get the address of your local Trust from the Royal Society for Nature Conservation, 22 The Green, Nettleham, Lincoln LN2 2NR. They will also give you information about the **WATCH** club – the junior branch of the Nature Conservation Trusts. **WATCH** has its own magazine, projects and local groups.

County or Local Natural History Societies. You can get the address of your local Society from CoEnCo, Zoological Gardens, Regents Park, London NW1. They plan programmes of talks and outings each year.

The Field Studies Council, Information Office, Preston Montford, Montford Bridge, Shrewsbury SY4 1HW. Runs outdoors courses in different aspects of natural history including wild flowers, held at its nine residential centres in Britain.

British Trust for Conservation Volunteers, 36 St Mary's Street, Wallingford, Oxon OX10 0EU, arrange task forces throughout Britain. You will learn most about the hard labour involved in tasks such as clearing scrub, but you will also learn about the habitat you are working on.

Books

The notes on pages 31–34 offer an introduction to the identification of flowers, but you will need a more comprehensive field guide. Here are some suggestions.

Flowers of Britain and Northern Europe by Fitter, Fitter and Blamey (Collins). Illustrations and short descriptions of each species.

The Excursion Flora of the British Isles by Clapham, Tutin and Warburg (Oxford University Press). No illustrations but detailed descriptions, with keys, of all species and their habitats.

These first two books work very well if used together.

Atlas of the Flowers of Britain and Northern Europe by Fitter (Collins) has maps showing where you could expect to find each species.

Usborne Guide to Wild Flowers by Barry Tebb (Usborne). Flowers arranged by colour.

The **New Naturalist** series, published by Collins, has some interesting titles such as **Flowers of Chalk and Limestone** and **Flowers of the Coast**. In these you will find full lists of the characteristic species of the different habitats. Also look out for books on the wild flowers or general natural history of your local area. These can give you useful background information about the area.

INDEX